SHORT ROMANCE KINDLE BOOKS

A COMPLETE GUIDE TO KINDLE PUBLISHING

NINA HARRINGTON

MORE RESOURCES FROM NINA

SUBSCRIBE HERE TO RECEIVE A FREE DIGITAL DOWNLOAD

HOW TO WRITE SHORT ROMANCE KINDLE BOOKS
A COMPLETE GUIDE TO KINDLE PUBLISHING
NINA HARRINGTON

THE 16-CHAPTER ROMANCE PLOT OUTLINE

A Complete Template with everything you need to Plot your own unique Romance Fiction.

Download a Free Text Copy of the 16-Chapter Romance Plot Template as a Welcome Gift when you Subscribe to my Newsletter.

Find out more here:
https://subscribepage.io/16CHAPTEROUTLINE

Contents

INTRODUCTION 5

PART ONE. UNDERSTANDING THE AMAZON KINDLE MARKET FOR ROMANCE FICTION 13

   1. Romance Fiction Categories and Niche Categories 20
   2. What is Your Niche? 25
   3. Writing to Market 28
   4. The Amazon Market for Short Fiction 45
   5. What are Romance Tropes? 56

PART TWO. CREATIVE WRITING 58

   6. Story Craft 59
   7. How to Develop Unforgettable Characters 64
   8. Conflict in Romance Fiction 72
   9. Dialogue and Point of View 78
   10. Setting and Sensuality 81

PART THREE. SELF-EDITING FOR ROMANCE WRITERS 85

   11. Storytelling and Story Structure - Two different things 86
   12. What is Emotional Story Structure? 94
   13. Story Structure for the Short Novel and Novella 97
   14. Story Structure for The Short Story 99
   15. Editing for Romance Writers 101

PART FOUR. BUILDING AN EBOOK 109

   16. The Practical Aspects of Building an eBook 110
   17. Book Cover Design 114
   18. Formatting your Manuscript into a Kindle eBook 121

PART FIVE. PUBLISHING ON AMAZON 146

19. PUBLISH YOUR EBOOK ON KDP 147
20. BOOK DESCRIPTIONS, KEYWORDS AND CATEGORIES 149
21. PRICING 160
22. PRE-ORDERS 165
23. KDP PRINT PAPERBACKS 168

PART SIX. MARKETING AND PROMOTION 175

24. PLANNING THE BOOK LAUNCH 176
25. AUTHOR BRANDING 185
26. AMAZON AUTHOR CENTRAL 187
27. EMAIL LIST BUILDING FOR ROMANCE AUTHORS 188
28. FREE MARKETING TOOLS AND TECHNIQUES 197
29. PAID MARKETING SERVICES 204
MORE RESOURCES FROM NINA 210
COPYRIGHT 212

INTRODUCTION

Hello! My name is Nina Harrington and I am the award-winning author of 19 romance and romantic mystery novels with sales of over one and a half million copies in 28 countries around the world in 23 languages.

But I know how hard it is to take that first step on the publishing ladder.

In 2002, I decided to take a leap of faith and leave my full-time career as an industrial scientist so that I could realise my dream and write the stories that I knew were burning inside of me.

As a scientist, I decided to learn everything I could about the craft of creating compelling genre fiction and the business aspects of being a professional author.

It was tough. When I started writing romance fiction, it was almost impossible to find training courses on commercial fiction and especially romance fiction.

It took me six years to win a contract with a major publisher and I had countless rejections along the way. My first novel, *Always the Bridesmaid*, was published by Harlequin Mills and Boon in July 2009 and is still one of my favourites.

When I started submitting romance fiction, most books were sold only in print format, paperback or hardback, from brick and mortar bookstores.

To reach those shelves in the bookstore, each book had to be approved by three levels of gatekeepers between the reader and the writer. First the literary agent, then the publisher, and in turn the bookseller who hand-sold the printed book.

There was a very clear vertical line with the writer at the bottom and the reader at the top.

Online booksellers were new. Digital books were very new.

Self-publishing carried the stigma of "vanity press" and was mocked as being the last resort for writers who could not find an agent or publisher who would invest in their work. But it was such a tiny piece of the book world and only their friends and family would buy the book anyway.

EVERY SINGLE ONE OF THOSE FACTS IS NO LONGER TRUE.

There has never been a better time to be a writer. *And there has never been a worse time to be a writer.*

I believe that statement is true whether you write commercial genre fiction as I do, or any other kind of fiction or non-fiction.

The English-speaking world has developed an insatiable hunger for the written word and demands to read those words on every kind of reading device created.

Dedicated eBook readers, desktop and laptop computers, smartphones and tablet devices with reading apps are part of our everyday lives.

Self-publishing has been made respectable and profitable by the large online booksellers who sell eBook readers and tablets such as Amazon, Kobo, Barnes and Noble and Apple.

It is in their interest to offer authors high royalties to publish material directly through them, especially in electronic format, where they get the cut the traditional publishers used to receive, and readers love them because they drive prices down.

And with digital eBooks you can be anywhere in the world and provided you have an internet connection, you can download the book you want in minutes and read it on a device you carry in your pocket.

Online booksellers also stock an enormous range of print titles, which would be impossible for any high street bookstore, and offer big discounts and free delivery to your door.

In response, traditional publishers have now introduced digital only, or digital first, publishing lines and many authors are now producing work for several publishers, in several genres at the same time under different pen names.

Brilliant! More markets for my quirky short stories, novellas, comics, journals and manuals that would never have found a traditional publisher! And you would be right to think that.

BUT ALL THAT MATERIAL CREATES A VERY SERIOUS PROBLEM.

The proliferation of reading devices and content has created such a deluge of material that the tidal wave has washed away traditional pricing structures for books.

The days when an author can write one fiction book a year and generate enough sales through a traditional publishing route are long gone. Unless you already have a huge fan-base who will pay for a hardback printed book, the income per book will be low and increasingly the sales figures will not support a publishing contract. And timing and accessibility is everything.

There is a glut of eBooks and readers expect to pay either very little for those books or even get them for free. This is especially true for genre fiction such as romance.

WHAT CAN WE DO AS AUTHORS TO BUILD CAREERS AS PUBLISHED AUTHORS?

We need to become more prolific and we need to be both educated and business-minded about what is the best publishing model for our work while trying to stand upright on the shifting sand that is today's publishing industry.

HOW DO THE TOP SELF-PUBLISHED FICTION AUTHORS MAKE MONEY?

By treating their writing as a business, where they are in control of every aspect of the book publishing process.

They are "authorpreneurs" who see their love of writing as a start-up business opportunity and are prepared to put in the hours of hard work to make it a successful business, however you define what that success looks like.

To become a successful romance author in the crowded romance marketplace, I believe that you must learn how to write, edit, produce, publish and promote your work so that readers know where to find it.

In other words, you need to develop the mindset of a book publisher.

This means releasing at least four to six books a year, preferably in a series, and slowly building a following so that the next book in the series, or a new series, becomes an auto-buy for readers.

That's one of the reasons why many romance authors prefer to write shorter romance fiction such as novellas and short novels.

In many cases, self-publishing may not be the best publishing model for your book project and skillset. If that is the case, there are numerous digital-first publishers and traditional publishers who will take over the publishing side of the business while you handle the writing, but you will still have to do a lot of the marketing and engage a literary agent to represent you.

That's why you must think carefully before going into self-publishing and make sure that you have the information and training you need to create an eBook or print-on-demand paperback that represents your story in the best possible way.

THAT IS NOT TO SAY THAT SELF-PUBLISHING IS AN EASY OPTION.

When a reader purchases your book, they want to enjoy a professionally produced romance story with the same quality standards that they would find in a printed book from a traditional publisher.

It is all too easy to feel overwhelmed by how much we have to know about story craft, editing, productivity, the publishing business, and how to become business savvy as a writer entrepreneur.

Building an author platform and readership take time and patience. This is not a quick and easy way to make money. You must accept that you are going to be in the Kindle publishing business for the long haul.

Most of the top romance authors have been writing and publishing for at least five to ten years, building up a back-list of books which are selling every day while they are working on the next new release.

For eBooks, it is now well established that if a reader loves one of your books, then they will want to purchase other books that you have created, especially if these books are linked in some way.

The books need to be online and available at that precise moment. Because if you don't have books available, then the moment is lost, and the reader with a short attention span will move on to the next author who does have a trilogy or more, all ready to be enjoyed. Right now. Speed is everything.

VISIBILITY AND PLATFORM = SALES.

Getting noticed in the romance publishing business has never been harder. Do not go down the self-publishing route unless you are prepared to invest a significant amount of time in marketing online and off. You will be fighting hard to attract your ideal reader in an extremely competitive marketplace.

You need to adopt an entrepreneurial attitude, drive, and the determination to make this work - but it is worth it.

Publishing a short romance eBook is not only doable but a proven and profitable way of sharing your work while generating long-term passive income.

Writing and self-publishing romance fiction has now become an ideal small business opportunity for many authors. It is an excellent option for home and part-time working or running as a side hustle business in addition to your day job.

Once your eBook is published it will never go out of print and you can continue to earn passive income without any additional production work – and it will be instantly distributed worldwide the moment you hit the publish button.

This is the digital world of self-publishing and Amazon Kindle Direct Publishing [KDP] leads the way.

SO HOW DO YOU WRITE AND SELF-PUBLISH SHORT ROMANCE KINDLE BOOKS?

I have created a detailed step by step plan which will give you the essential information you need to write your own romance fiction and then build those stories into eBooks which can be published through KDP.

This book covers the Four Clear Stages in the Kindle Publishing Cycle.

CONCEPT AND STORY IDEA.

Do you have an audience for the romance story that you want to write? Develop a clear understanding of the current Amazon market and select specific and strategic Amazon categories or niches for your romance fiction.

CREATE.

The actual writing process. This book recommends a proven, six-layer character development process to help you to create compelling three-dimensional characters who readers will love! Then self-editing techniques for the ideal word count for your book.

SELF-PUBLISHING ON THE AMAZON KINDLE PLATFORM.

The Practical Aspects of Building an eBook. This includes detailed step by step instructions on how to format and layout your manuscript before you upload the document onto the KDP platform.

PROMOTION.

Including building an author brand, email list building and making connections with readers.

Are you ready to build a profitable business writing and selling romance Kindle eBooks? Then let's get started! I promise it will be quite a journey!

PART ONE. UNDERSTANDING THE AMAZON KINDLE MARKET FOR ROMANCE FICTION

Understanding the Amazon Kindle Market for Romance Fiction

Have you ever read a totally enthralling romance novel and been so carried away with the characters and their love story, that when you turned the last page you asked yourself: "*I wonder if I could write romance like that?*"

The good news for writers is there has never been a better time to create your own romance stories and find readers who will enjoy them. In fact, romance fiction publishing has grown into what is now a billion-dollar publishing industry.

Although mystery, thriller and crime fiction are the most popular book genres in the US, romance and erotic fiction makes the most money at **$1.44 billion.** [Source. BookAdReport.]

1.44 billion dollars. And this data is a few years out of date. It is probably a lot more now.

Romance readers were among the first to take to electronic books and have shifted much of their buying over to it.

This trend has continued and there is strong evidence that fiction is more popular for digital downloads and e-readers. [Source. Markinblog.]

It is little wonder that romance is the top performing category on the best-seller lists and represents the highest earning category for self-published authors on Amazon.

Romance is the top selling fiction genre on the Amazon.com Kindle store [USA] with about 900,000 titles available and this has increased by over 22% from October 2020 to October 2021. Romance titles are very high ranking, and the sales performance has been both extremely stable over the past five years and actually benefited overall from the impact of the Pandemic.

Don't forget that romance and women's fiction is also published as secondary themes within the other main genres such as Literature and Fiction, Mystery, Thriller and Suspense, Religion and Spirituality and Teen and Young Adult, so the actual sales figure for the romance genre is actually much higher.

Sales of romance have never been higher, and readers are looking for romance fiction of all genres and lengths to satisfy their compulsion for this genre.

WHAT MAKES ROMANCE FICTION SO POPULAR WITH READERS? THE RANGE OF SUB-GENRES AVAILABLE.

One of the reasons for the universal popularity of romance fiction is that there is now a huge range of story lines for readers to enjoy, covering the full spectrum of sensuality and settings, themes and story ideas to meet the tastes of every reader.

For example, there are currently 102 romance sub-genres listed on Amazon.com, and new niche markets are being added every year. Romance fiction may be set in a contemporary or historical time period, have a mystery or thriller plot, be set in any setting, including fantasy and science fiction locations and be meshed with added layers of sensuality from inspirational sweet to extremely hot romantic erotica.

This diversity means that there truly is a romance story for every audience – and for any writer.

Romance fiction offers writers very special opportunities to explore stories and characters which are as unique as their imagination can take them.

But that enormous diversity creates a problem.

Image credit: flickr/pfala

Imagine walking into a bookstore and finding stacks of books of all types all piled up together without any kind of order. It would be impossible to find the book you are looking for without sorting through hundreds of random books.

Now is the time to ask yourself two key questions:

• **Why do you want to write romance, and**

• **What kind of romance do you love to read and write?**

WHY DO YOU WANT TO WRITE SHORT ROMANCE KINDLE BOOKS?

Be honest with yourself.

How you approach writing on Kindle depends on understanding the reason why you want to release your work on this online platform and the amount of work that you are prepared to undertake to make it as successful as you able.

• Do you want to make a living from your Kindle books as side-hustle or a full-time business?

• Do you want to make a mark on society with a unique style or commentary? Perhaps to leave a legacy with the stories that you have been burning to tell.

• Do you simply enjoy writing for its own sake and want to share your stories around the world and the sales are a bonus?

• Or something else? Is this a fun experiment with something new and exciting?

• Do you believe that you are writing for yourself and then hope other romance book readers will discover your work when the book is finished?

Every romance author begins their journey as a reader first, then someone who enjoys writing romance as a hobby.

The next step on that journey may be self-publishing on Kindle as you develop your skills and use your talent to create compelling fiction.

Other authors make the decision to use Kindle eBooks to build a business based around their talent and love of a particular genre of romance.

There is no right or wrong path. This has to your individual journey.

But one thing is true.

Way too many romance authors write the book they want to write and THEN think about how they are going to share that book, market and promote their work and hopefully persuade friends and family to leave a review on the Amazon book page.

This only leads to frustration and disappointment and more than a little heartbreak.

> *"Hope" eBook marketing is not a strategy for success, however you define success to be.*

A far better way is to know in advance that there are readers for the romance that you love to read and want to write, and you have the tools and techniques which will help your work to be discovered by ideal readers.

Self-publishing any book requires a significant investment in time and money and most of the process has nothing to do with creative writing.

You must become the publisher and learn everything from story craft through to formatting and cover design and then marketing, building an author platform, and promoting your email list.

Every part of this process takes time, energy and money from the start.

Many romance authors sadly give up on their dream of sharing their romance fiction because the publishing process is too demanding, and they don't have the energy and funds to make it work.

So, how badly do you want this?

How much time can you invest in publishing your work? One hour a day is a great place to start but you can achieve a lot more than you imagine in thirty-minute sessions.

Question. Is there an audience for your work?

Answer. Almost certainly.

The remarkably high ranking of romance titles is proof of that, across all the sub-genres. And there are many niche romance sub-genres which are not too crowded. But we are still talking about thousands of books and there are more being added to every bestseller list every day.

Whatever your reason, this book focuses on the tools and techniques you need to write and publish the most compelling romance fiction – and then share your work with the largest ideal audience.

Righty. *Let's get our business head on*.

1. Romance Fiction Categories and Niche Categories

Amazon places romance eBooks onto virtual bookshelves in the Kindle Store called categories, which are broadly equivalent to romance sub-genres, with a lot of cross-over.

The main categories are broadly the same as you would find in a brick and mortar high street bookstore, but no bookstore in the world can stock at least 900,000 English romance titles.

These combinations of setting and plot mean that romance fiction is currently listed in 102 romance subcategories and sub-subcategories in the Amazon.com Kindle store.

The main Romance category alone breaks down into 51 subcategories.

Subcategories exist so that readers can browse the online shelves to find the latest releases in the kind of story they love to read the most and easily find other romance books with the same combinations of settings, tone and plot distinctions that characterise that subgenre.

What "virtual bookshelf" is your book going to sit on?

The huge advantage of this wide range of subcategories is that any romance reader is going to find precisely the kind of story that they are looking for. From paranormal vampire romance to inspirational historical Amish romance, there will be a niche on the Amazon store– and new niches are being added every year.

Given the huge number of romance titles currently available, it is essential that any romance writer who wants to publish on the

Amazon Kindle Direct Publishing [KDP] platform is able to clearly define precisely which niche they are going to target with their work.

THERE ARE SEVEN MAIN AMAZON CATEGORIES WHICH CONTAIN ROMANCE FICTION.

These are:

1. Romance. The main Romance category.
2. Literature and Fiction. Including Erotic Romance, Women's Fiction and Short Stories.
3. Science Fiction and Fantasy.
4. Teen and Young Adult.
5. Religion and Spirituality.
6. LGBTQ+ [Lesbian, Gay, Bisexual and Transgender.]
7. Comics, Manga and Graphic Novels.

THE MAIN ROMANCE CATEGORY

Within this main Romance Kindle category, there are twenty-five major subcategories and twenty-three smaller sub-subcategory romance submarkets currently listed on the Amazon.com Kindle Store.

The major Romance subcategories are:

- Action & Adventure
- Anthologies
- Clean & Wholesome
- Collections & Anthologies
- Contemporary
- Fantasy
- Gothic
- Historical Romance
- Holidays
- Inspirational
- LGBTQ+ Romance

- Later in Life
- Medical
- Military
- Multicultural & Interracial
- Mystery & Suspense
- New Adult & College
- Paranormal
- Rockstar Romance
- Romance
- Romantic Comedy
- Science Fiction
- Sports
- Time Travel
- Westerns

ADDITIONAL CATEGORIES THAT CONTAIN ROMANCE

LITERATURE & FICTION

Within this main category, there are several subcategories currently listed which include romance and women's fiction including:

• Literary Fiction: Action and Adventure: Romance

• Literary Fiction: Black and African American: Romance

• Literary Fiction: Contemporary Fiction: Romance

• Literary Fiction: Classics: Romance

• Literary Fiction: Women's Fiction: Romance

• There are 18 sub-subcategories for Erotica, including Erotic Romance and

• 16 types of Short Stories.

FANTASY AND SCIENCE FICTION

This is a wide category with almost 50 sub-subcategories covering everything from romance to paranormal and urban to new adult to short stories. Plenty of scope!

TEEN AND YOUNG ADULT

The Kindle Store Teen and Young Adult Romance subcategory has eight sub-subcategories which include romance fiction:

- Clean and Wholesome
- Contemporary
- Historical Fiction
- Mysteries and Thrillers/Romantic
- Paranormal and Fantasy,
- Romantic Comedy
- Science Fiction and Dystopian and
- Lesbian, Gay, Bisexual and Transgender.

RELIGION AND SPIRITUALITY

Religious Fiction includes:

- Christian Fiction/Romance
- Romance
- Women's Fiction
- Short Stories.

There are multiple niche markets within this broad category.

LESBIAN, GAY, BISEXUAL & TRANSGENDER EBOOKS

<u>Lesbian, Gay, Bisexual & Transgender eBooks</u> include a wide range of subcategories, covering most forms of genre fiction, including Erotica and Romance, Mystery and Science Fiction.

COMICS AND GRAPHIC NOVELS

<u>Graphic Novels</u> include subcategories for:

• Contemporary Women

• Erotica

• Romance

***

There are also romantic elements and subplots in many mainstream novels and crime fiction novels which are not included in these categories.

Hopefully, you can now appreciate why romance fiction is one of the most inclusive and wide-ranging genre fiction forms for both readers and writers.

Niche markets that would never be published by traditional publishing houses have found new readers through online publishing platforms such as KDP. In the same way, writers have been able to create the kind of niche book they love to read, but could not find in a traditional bookstore, and then share that work worldwide.

You should be aware that new subgenres can emerge at any time and become popular while others fade. But that is the power of romance fiction. It is constantly changing and adapting.

2. What is Your Niche?

To succeed in self-publishing, you need to be very clear about which section of the romance eBook market you are going to compete in.

You may have to drill down several layers to find the perfect match for the book that you want to write and fully appreciate what readers are looking for in that niche.

Your target readers are looking for a specific type of book and can describe it in the same terms that Amazon uses.

Paranormal romance, for example, is way too broad a segment of the romance market. A better example would be Angels, Paranormal Romance, or Reverse Harem Paranormal Romance.

It is essential that you clearly understand the Amazon niche categories before you write your Kindle romance.

Why?

#1. Discoverability.

#2. So you can shape the story you are burning to write into a form that your ideal readers will love.

There are thousands of new romance titles being published every week on the Amazon Kindle store.

Publishing any book is hard and marketing that book is even tougher. It is crucial that you educate yourself and understand the current market for your romance fiction as soon as you have an idea for a short romance story.

HOW TO LEVERAGE THE POWER OF AMAZON CATEGORIES TO HELP READERS FIND YOUR WORK

To a reader, Amazon Kindle Store and other online bookstores are the best equivalent to mega bricks and mortar bookstores with limitless supplies of any published book, anywhere, at anytime, anywhere in the world. It is truly magical.

Self-published authors know that online book platforms are more than that. *They are powerful search engines.*

Your Kindle eBook is simply a numbered data file linked to an image. A piece of code which has associated words attached to it. Those words are **the metadata** for your book; the title, subtitle, book description, the two categories you assign to your book, the price and the seven keyword strings, plus any publisher information and an ISBN if you are using one. It is the combination of all these details that makes the book unique.

Readers must know that your work exists before they can admire your quality book cover and buy and read your romance.

Question. How can you help your ideal reader to find your book on the virtual shelves?

Answer. By being strategic from the start and writing the romance story that you want to write, but with a clear understanding of how and where the audience for that story is going to find your work.

In other words, you must know the subcategories or sub-subcategories where your romance is going to shelved on the Kindle store.

Too many fiction authors write the book of their heart and then look around to see where they can place it so that they can share it with the world.

A romance novella or short romance novel can take several months to write, edit, revise, source a cover design and then publish online. That investment in time and money should be rewarded with sales and positive reviews.

There are several ways that any self-published author can leverage the power of the Amazon Kindle online search engine to help a reader find their romance book.

For both keywords and categories, the Amazon ranking of your book is calculated using a complex and secret algorithm.

Your goal should always be to rank within specific Kindle categories. That's why optimizing for keyword and category ranking is the most effective ways to market your romance long term.

Question. Why is this so important for romance eBook publishers?

Answer. Your sales income = [the number of books you sell] x [the royalty payment for that eBook].

The number of books you sell is impacted by several factors including cover design, the quality of the content, and how you have described and set-up your sales information on the online bookstore.

Most important of all?

Ranking well on the Kindle Store allows your content to get discovered organically by readers long after you put in initial marketing effort.

3. Writing to Market

There are many very successful romance authors who have recognised a trend in popularity in the Kindle store in a particular romance sub-genre and have story ideas and characters which will work in that type of romance eBook.

These authors have strategically decided to "write to market" and deliberately shape their book so that it will fit into a sub-genre which is currently very popular.

They know that the audience exists for this kind of eBook and that they can get extra visibility and sales by following the trend. Their goals are to be listed on bestselling chart position, in the Hot New Releases for a subcategory AND in the first 20 search results for that niche Kindle bookstore.

The romance story still must be well-crafted with compelling characters, so that readers will enjoy the work, but it also has to meet the genre expectations of that particular sub-genre.

Growing Niche Romance Markets.

One example of this is the recent addition of a completely new Romance Category – **Rockstar Romance**.

Other categories have attracted new readers. For example, K-Lytics reports that the sales rank of **Sports Romance** bestsellers have increased by 41% in the past 12 months (April 2022 to April 2023.)

Over the same period, the average Amazon Kindle Sales Rank of the top 20 **Western Romance** bestsellers increased by 29%, and **Contemporary Romance** by 12%.

At the same time, the average Amazon Kindle sales rank for **Romance Anthologies** has dropped by more than 145% over the past year.

THE DANGER OF WRITING TO MARKET

The popularity of certain romance markets can shift very quickly, so only write the story that you want to write, but with your eyes wide open to how and where you are going to place it.

You have to love reading and writing that kind of story. That is a given. After all, you are going to be building up an audience and a following for your work online and your readers will expect you to continue writing in that sub-genre, even if it is not as popular as it was six months ago.

I am not saying that writing to market is the only way to be successful. Far from it. But it is one example of authors who have proactively identified that there is an audience for their work in advance, they enjoy writing those stories, and they have stories which will fit that sub-genre.

They know that there is an audience for their work, so they are not "writing into the blue" then hoping that someone will buy and read their eBook apart from their friends and family.

HOW COMPETITIVE IS YOUR NICHE?

You should always focus on two things:

Factor #1. What subgenre is the most relevant and the best fit for the books you love to read and write. Where can you find the kind of romances that you love to read? Where are they placed on the Kindle store?

Factor #2. How competitive that category is. There are currently approximately one million Romance Kindle titles on Amazon.com.

How many other eBooks are published in your chosen category?

This should give you an indication of the level of demand for your kind of book. For example, Contemporary Romance, Romantic Suspense and Romantic Comedy lead subcategory sales in Romance, but there is huge competition in these genres.

The section that follows is a brief guide about how to analyse how competitive each of the major romance subcategories are, so that you have a good understanding of how the Kindle Market works.

A quick way to calculate how hard it would be to dominate a category is see how much competition there is within that category, which is reflected in the ranking of the books in that category.

Go onto the Amazon.com home page, then use the drop-down menu to go to the Kindle Store, then the Kindle eBooks tab, then Bestsellers on the top line menu.

This takes you to the main page for all of the categories which are listed on the left side of the page.

• Click on the main category which is the best fit for the kind of book you are looking for and take a look at the options available.

• Choose one subcategory, if there is one, where you know that similar books to yours have been published and scan the bestseller list.

• Then make a note of the following facts. What is the ranking of the top book, the number 20 book and then number 100 book in that bestselling chart?

The lower the rank, the more popular the book. The bestseller ranking is basically an indication of how many books are selling *better* than yours.

Here is a snapshot of the **Amazon Bestseller Ranking** details of the top 100 books in each of **the main Romance subcategories on Amazon.com Kindle Store**, listed alphabetically - as of April 2023.

IMPORTANT. The rankings are updated every hour, so the information below must be taken as a snapshot of what is happening on a particular day in that moment, but it will give you enough information for you to gauge how relatively crowded and competitive that subcategory is. Always check the latest data for the category that you are interested in.

ACTION AND ADVENTURE

Estimated Number of Titles in this Sub-Category: 11,298

Ranking of Book 1: 103

Ranking of Book 20: 2,076

Ranking of Book 100: 10,711

CLEAN & WHOLESOME

Estimated Number of Titles in this Sub-Category: 14,500

Ranking of Book 1: 611

Ranking of Book 20: 3,967

Ranking of Book 100: 12,382

COLLECTIONS & ANTHOLOGIES

Estimated Number of Titles in this Sub-Category: 22,700

Ranking of Book 1: 1,049

Ranking of Book 20: 4,300

Ranking of Book 100: 18,310

CONTEMPORARY

Estimated Number of Titles in this Sub-Category: 300,000

Ranking of Book 1: 1

Ranking of Book 20: 41

Ranking of Book 100: 234

FANTASY

Estimated Number of Titles in this Sub-Category: 74,364

Ranking of Book 1: 42

Ranking of Book 20: 295

Ranking of Book 100: 1,118

GOTHIC

Estimated Number of Titles in this Sub-Category: 5,826

Ranking of Book 1: 11

Ranking of Book 20: 1,320

Ranking of Book 100: 7,330

HISTORICAL ROMANCE

Includes a range of small niche markets, including: <u>Ancient World, Medieval, Regency, Scottish, and Victorian and the new sub-markets Tudor, Renaissance and American</u>

Estimated Number of Titles in this Sub-Category: 90,980

Ranking of Book 2: 176

Ranking of Book 20: 1,083

Ranking of Book 100: 4,765

HOLIDAYS

Estimated Number of Titles in this Sub-Category: 38,260

Ranking of Book 1: 136

Ranking of Book 21: 2,988

Ranking of Book 100: 17,748

INSPIRATIONAL

Estimated Number of Titles in this Sub-Category: 91,450

Ranking of Book 1: 231

Ranking of Book 20: 1,352

Ranking of Book 100: 5,419

LATER IN LIFE

Estimated Number of Titles in this Sub-Category: 2,326

Ranking of Book 1: 622

Ranking of Book 20: 13,357

Ranking of Book 100: 47,371

LGBT [LESBIAN, GAY, BISEXUAL AND TRANSGENDER]

Includes Romance -Bisexual Romance, Gay Romance -Lesbian Romance. Transgender Romance

Estimated Number of Titles in this Sub-Category: 97,600

Ranking of Book 1: 6

Ranking of Book 20: 1,199

Ranking of Book 100: 4,322

MEDICAL

Estimated Number of Titles in this Sub-Category: 2,670

Ranking of Book 1: 488

Ranking of Book 20: 14,286

Ranking of Book 100: 90,061

MILITARY

Estimated Number of Titles in this Sub-Category: 33,277

Ranking of Book 1: 26

Ranking of Book 20: 725

Ranking of Book 100: 3,407

MULTICULTURAL & INTERRACIAL

Estimated Number of Titles in this Sub-Category: 34,256

Ranking of Book 1: 1

Ranking of Book 20: 3,171

Ranking of Book 100: 6,430

MYSTERY & SUSPENSE

Estimated Number of Titles in this Sub-Category: 106,550

Ranking of Book 1: 19

Ranking of Book 20: 191

Ranking of Book 100: 849

NEW ADULT & COLLEGE

This fairly recent subgenre is now emerging for slightly older characters aged 17 to early twenties. These are readers who grew up with Young Adult Romance and are now looking for a more sensually charged romance to match their lives.

Estimated Number of Titles in this Sub-Category: 26,236

Ranking of Book 1: 33

Ranking of Book 20: 351

Ranking of Book 100: 2,258

PARANORMAL

This is a large subcategory with seven sub-sub categories: Angels, Demons & Devils, Ghosts, Psychics, Vampires, Werewolves & Shifters, Witches & Wizards

Urban Fantasy Romance is usually included under this subcategory.

Estimated Number of Titles in this Sub-Category: 110,300

Ranking of Book 1: 5

Ranking of Book 20: 353

Ranking of Book 100: 1,431

ROCKSTAR ROMANCE

This is a brand new romance subcategory as of April 2023, with less than 5,000 titles. No detailed information is available.

Ranking of Book 1: 422

Ranking of Book 20: 28,658

Ranking of Book 100: 200,787

ROMANTIC COMEDY

Estimated Number of Titles in this Sub-Category: 102,324

Ranking of Book 1: 2

Ranking of Book 20: 114

Ranking of Book 100: 763

SCIENCE FICTION

Estimated Number of Titles in this Sub-Category: 29,300

Ranking of Book 1: 166

Ranking of Book 20: 1,486

Ranking of Book 100: 5,413

SPORTS

Estimated Number of Titles in this Sub-Category: 27,192

Ranking of Book 1: 6

Ranking of Book 20: 175

Ranking of Book 100: 1,505

TIME TRAVEL

Estimated Number of Titles in this Sub-Category: 7,333

Ranking of Book 1: 372

Ranking of Book 20: 9,999

Ranking of Book 100: 27,476

WESTERNS

Estimated Number of Titles in this Sub-Category: 28,327

Ranking of Book 1: 66

Ranking of Book 20: 1,187

Ranking of Book 100: 5,513

As you can see, there is a huge variation between subcategories, from the tiny **Medical** or **Later in Life** Romance lists, to the competitive Contemporary list which has over a quarter of a million titles.

HOW TO ESTIMATE THE NUMBER OF TITLES IN A SPECIFIC NICHE

NOTE: Amazon used to display the number of books in each category. That information is now no longer provided.

What you CAN do is drill down to an individual niche sub-subcategory and then **click on one of the Romantic Themes or Hero Types for that niche**. The number of titles in that niche will be displayed for that combination at the top of the page.

For example. Let's say that you are writing a Clean and Wholesome short romance novel set around a wedding planner who has been hired by wealthy aristocrats.

#1. Go to the Amazon.com store and click on the Kindle Store option then leave the search box empty.

#2. Then click on the Kindle eBooks option in the left sidebar.

#3. Then click on the Romance category.

#4. Click on Clean and Wholesome. At the top of the main results page there will be a banner displaying the approximate number of books in that sub-subcategory: Kindle Store : Kindle eBooks : Romance : Clean & Wholesome. In this case there are over 10,000 titles available.

amazon
Kindle Store
Deliver to RAY-ANNE Basingstoke RG21 5NX
Today's Deals
RAYANNE's Amazon.com
Buy a Kindle
Kindle eBooks
Kindle Unlimited
Prime Reading
Show results for
Kindle Unlimited
Kindle Unlimited Eligible
Prime Reading
Prime Reading Eligible
Great on Kindle
Great on Kindle Eligible
Audible Narration
eBooks with Audible Narration
New Releases
Last 30 days
Last 90 days
Coming Soon
Kindle Store
Kindle Newsstand
Kindle Newspapers
Kindle Short Reads
Kindle Singles
Kindle eBooks
Kindle Store
Mother's Day Week: Top
When We Believed in Mermaids: A Novel
Barbara O'Neal
Kindle Edition
(6,080)
Amazon Charts: Most So

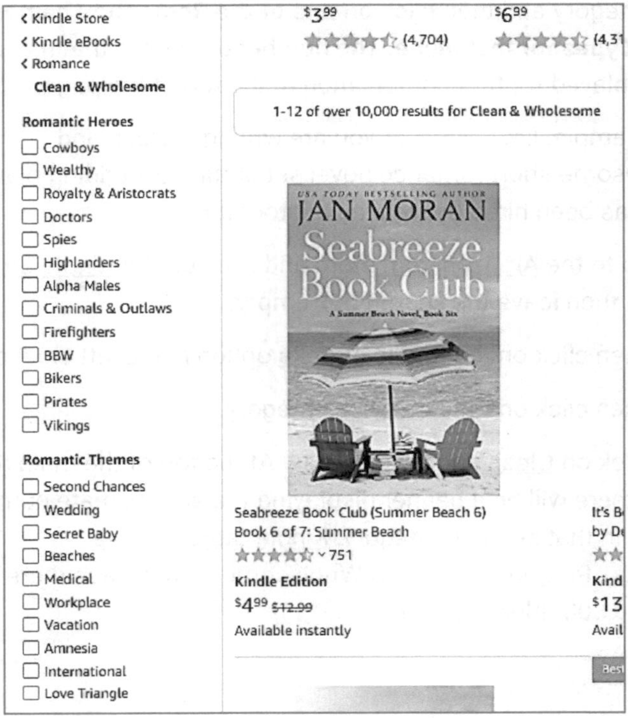
Kindle Store
Kindle eBooks
Romance
Clean & Wholesome
Romantic Heroes
Cowboys
Wealthy
Royalty & Aristocrats
Doctors
Spies
Highlanders
Alpha Males
Criminals & Outlaws
Firefighters
BBW
Bikers
Pirates
Vikings
Romantic Themes
Second Chances
Wedding
Secret Baby
Beaches
Medical
Workplace
Vacation
Amnesia
International
Love Triangle
$3.99
(4,704)
$6.99
1-12 of over 10,000 results for Clean & Wholesome
USA TODAY BESTSELLING AUTHOR
JAN MORAN
Seabreeze Book Club
A Summer Beach Novel, Book Six
Seabreeze Book Club (Summer Beach 6)
Book 6 of 7: Summer Beach
751
Kindle Edition
$4.99 $12.99
Available instantly

#5. You can then refine your search by clicking on the type of Romantic Hero or Romantic Theme that describes your book. In this example, click on the Wedding Romantic Theme. This reduces the number of search results to over 1,000 books.

#6. You can then refine your search further by clicking on the type of Romantic hero in this book: Wealthy and Royalty and Aristocrats.

Much better – you now have **50 books which meet those search criteria**: Kindle Store : Kindle eBooks : Romance : Clean & Wholesome : Wedding : Wealthy and Royalty & Aristocrats.

There is a great chance that this book will be discovered if you add those search categories and keywords into your book details.

Clearly this is a small niche and for larger categories such as Contemporary Romance there will be a large number of search results. For example. There are 746 results for Kindle eBooks : Romance : Contemporary : Wedding : Wealthy and Royalty & Aristocrats.

You can continue refining your search in this way for any subcategory until you can drill down to the specific combination of niche description, type of romantic hero and romantic theme which are a great fit for your book.

HOW TO INTERPRET THE ROMANCE CATEGORY BESTSELLER CHARTS

Question. Why is it important to know all these numbers and do all this research?

Answer. Imagine that each category has a virtual bookshelf.

Where would your book fit on that shelf? Is there room for it? Or would it be pushed to the back by all of the big-name popular authors who will dominate the charts?

AMOUNT OF COMPETITION BETWEEN CATEGORIES

Romance is a big and competitive genre. There are more than 900,000 English titles on Kindle. And the influx of new romance books being published every week seems unstoppable. It really is a balancing act between accurate classification and competition.

What you find when you look closer at the books in the top 20 bestsellers for each category is that the same books are often listed in more than one category.

You want your book to be in a bestselling chart on Amazon so that readers can easily find it.

This means that your ideal category would be one where the top 100 books are not so popular, and the book ranking is high – that is to say, the books are not so popular and other books are selling faster.

I know that means that the sales figures are lower, but in the long term that can work in your favour.

But at the same time your book has to be stacked on a shelf which is the best fit for the content and romance subgenre.

So how do you balance these two factors?

- Select one main category that is the best fit or your romance.
- Select a second category which is similar but where there are fewer books to compete against.

Example One: You want to write a sweet contemporary novella set around the Christmas holiday period.

Your Main Category is Contemporary Romance.

This is the mainstay of the romance eBook market and the sales figures and popularity of these titles reflect that fact. Contemporary romance books will dominate the top 100 of all of the bestselling print and digital charts in the US and include all of the top romance authors.

Estimated Number of Titles in the Contemporary Romance Subcategory =300,000 and the top 100 bestsellers have low bestseller rankings. Ranking of Book 100: 234

The competition is therefore extremely high and even with a quality eBook it is going to be tough to beat the New York major publishing houses who want to be in the top 100 bestseller Contemporary Romance Chart.

But is it possible to include your book in a Second Category which has less competition?

What if your romance is set during a Holiday Period?

This subcategory could be a great choice for a contemporary romance which includes a holiday setting such as Christmas or the summer vacation.

Estimated Number of Titles in the Holiday Romance Sub-Category: 38,260. Ranking of Book 100= 17,748.

Could it be described as having a Clean and Wholesome Theme?

Estimated Number of Titles in the Clean & Wholesome Subcategory: 14,500. Ranking of Book 100=12,382.

A clean and wholesome romance book with a ranking of around 12,000 is selling around 15 copies a day*, while a contemporary book with a ranking of 234 means that on average it is being downloaded around 440 times a day.*

[*https://kindlepreneur.com/amazon-kdp-sales-rank-calculator/]

But compare the amount of competition for the top 100 titles.

Your book has more chance of being discovered by readers if it is listed in a subcategory with few titles such as Holiday Romance and Clean and Wholesome.

Example Two: You want to write an Historical Romance set in Scotland with a time-slip hero.

The success of TV shows such as `Outlander' which is adapted from the best-selling books by Diana Gabaldon has consolidated interest in Scottish Historical Romance and Time Slip/Time Travel.

Estimated Number of Titles in the Historical Romance Subcategory: 90,980. Ranking of Book 100=4,765.

An eBook with a rank of 4.760 is selling around 38 books a day.

Estimated Number of Titles in the Time Travel Romance Subcategory: 7,333. Ranking of Book 100= 27,476.

An eBook with a rank of 27,476 is selling around 11 books a day.

So, you would definitely be more likely to be discovered if you place your book in these smaller niche categories such as Historical Romance: Scottish and Time Travel Romance.

Yes, the sales will be modest, but fans of these books are voracious readers who will come to the Kindle Store looking for more Scottish time travel romances.

If they love your work and you can write a linked series, then you can quickly build up a solid author platform.

You can use this approach with any subcategory to determine the amount of competition your book will face and where can you place your work to attract your ideal readers.

HOW DOES RANKING COMPARE WITH SALES AND DOWNLOADS?

It is clearly not a linear scale!

eBook Ranking on Amazon.com	Estimated eBook Sales a Day
30,000	10
20,000	13
10,000	15
5,000	34
3,000	70
2,000	90
500	175

Sales figures calculated using the Kindlepreneur calculation tool - https://kindlepreneur.com/amazon-kdp-sales-rank-calculator/

4. The Amazon Market for Short Fiction

WHAT DO WE MEAN BY <u>SHORT</u> ROMANCE FICTION?

How do you like to read romance fiction?

Do you look for a short story in a magazine? Or a novella which only takes an hour or two to read? Perhaps you prefer to read in private on your smartphone, tablet computer or eBook reader?

Short romance stories fit the shift to reading on small hand-held devices perfectly.

• **Short stories range from 3,000 up to 7,500 words in length.**

• **Novelettes from 7,500 - 19,000 words.**

• **Novellas from 20,000 to 40,000 words.**

• **Short Romance novels from 40,000 upwards depending on the subgenre.**

In contrast, most commercial romance novels from traditional publishers are between 60,000 and 100,000 words in length. Novels longer than this fall into the 'epic' or 'saga' category.

This shift in reading habits using new technology means that many readers are now downloading shorter length stories which can be read and enjoyed on the commute to work or over a lunch break. Short fiction is perfect for those precious brief opportunities to read for pleasure which we squeeze into our busy lives.

A reader might not want to invest their time on a full- length novel or 100,000-word sagas which they know that they will only be able to sample in short 30 minute or one-hour slots at most. They prefer to dive in and enjoy a complete story over a break or an afternoon.

Short fiction is also a great way for readers to discover an author and sample their work at a low cost and therefore low risk.

This move to new ways of consuming romance fiction is set to continue, driving demand for more short form romance fiction.

WHY WORD COUNT MATTERS

Just as there are numerous subgenres of romance fiction, romance writers can tell their stories in as many, or as few, words as they choose.

Stories are classified according to the number of words in the piece. This is known as the "wordcount" of the story and it is usually interpreted as the computer wordcount on your word processing software.

It is important to remember that when you are writing your romance fiction, you should <u>always allow the story to dictate how many words it needs</u> to be told in the best way possible.

There are many authors who started off writing a short story and ended up with a piece with 25,000 words which was perfect as a novella. And that is just what should happen!

Short romance fiction is also a great format for authors who want to experiment with new genres and niche romance settings and subcategories. They can test whether they love writing in these new genres and how readers respond to their work.

Many authors have multiple pen names so that they are free to experiment and have fun!

Here are the general guidelines for romance fiction. You will notice that there is a lot of overlap between the very broad categories.

Here is an approximate guideline for story lengths.

FLASH FICTION. USUALLY 1,000 TO 2,000 WORDS

Flash Fiction is a very short story around the 1,500 words. Just long enough to be complete but short enough to hold attention. These stories would normally be sold electronically in e-magazines or collections with a linked common theme.

SHORT STORIES. 3,000 UP TO 7,000 WORDS

Determining what exactly separates a short story from longer formats is problematic. A classic definition of a short story is that one should be able to read it in one sitting.

The exact word count has been inherited from the world of print publishing. One publisher may specify a maximum word count of, for example, 7,000 words but another prefers a shorter piece of 4,000 words or even shorter for magazine pieces.

Although these restrictions no longer apply to electronic publishing, a reader will still expect to experience a complete story experience in one short piece.

It will usually take place in one setting with the hero and heroine and a minimal cast of secondary characters and will have to be very tightly structured and expressively written to deliver a powerful emotional experience for the reader in few words.

THE NOVELETTE. 7,500 - 19,000 WORDS

The next step up from short stories. This is one area where electronic publishing has made it possible to share more rounded stories with an audience who are looking for a short, intense and deeply immersive story which is quick to read.

Traditional publishers have offered collections of extended short stories in print, but these tended to be in restricted subgenres. Online publishing now makes it possible to write and distribute novelettes in any subgenre, either singly or in collected box sets.

Let your imagination go wild! Explore ideas and test the market.

THE NOVELLA. 20,000 TO 40,000 WORDS

This length of romance fiction has become very popular in digital publishing since it is easily read in a short time in electronic format.

Novella length romance fiction can be found in every romance subgenre and secondary genres such as Literary Fiction, which includes erotic romance, and Religion and Spirituality, where clean and wholesome short romance is always in demand.

LGBT authors, for example, have found exciting new ways of sharing their work as novella length romance stories.

Collections of linked novellas are popular with readers who love series fiction and offer writers another format for their work.

SHORT NOVEL. 40,000 TO 56,000 WORDS

The Romance Writers of America classify Short Contemporary Romance novels as being between 40,000 to 56,000 words, and Short **Historical Romance** Novels as between 40,000 and 89,000 words. [https://www.rwa.org/page/rita-rules]

This short novel classification includes the "category romance" novels published in monthly series by traditional publishers such as Harlequin/Harper Collins and many digital-first publishing companies.

Short romance novels on Kindle are usually between 40,000 and 60,000 words in length, depending on the subgenre of the romance story, but the trend is now towards shorter digital short novels when they are published electronically. This longer format allows writers the space to add in secondary characters, space for more and one locations and deeper character arcs for the romance couple.

WHAT EFFECT DOES THE LENGTH OF THE STORY HAVE WHEN PUBLISHING ON THE AMAZON KINDLE STORE?

Amazon has an extra special section for short fiction in the Kindle Store on the main Amazon home page called **Kindle Short Reads**.

It is not intended to replace the main categories we have already covered. Instead this is an extra collection that pulls together shorter fiction from the other categories into one place. The goal is simple – to help readers find the short fiction they love as quickly as possible.

> **Kindle Store**
> Kindle Newsstand
> Kindle Newspapers
> Kindle Short Reads
> Kindle Singles
> Kindle eBooks

Books are classified according to the estimated number of virtual pages in the file, creating six libraries of short read books.

EBooks on Kindle don't have actual page counts or word count. This is because there is no "page" in electronic files – the mobi file is one continuous piece of code which is formatted using the instructions you provide. In addition, most Kindle devices and readers allow you to increase the font size which will increase the number of pages in a document.

For an eBook that does **not have a print edition**, Amazon KDP states: "The estimated length is calculated using the number of page turns on a Kindle using settings to closely represent a physical book."

This corresponds to the following Kindle settings:

Font size: smallest

Typeface: condensed

Line Spacing: small

Words per Line: default

Estimates vary based on different Kindle devices available, but the above settings translate into **approximately 250-300 words per typed page on average**.

Short Reads: Great Stories in One Sitting
Browse by Reading Time: 15 minutes | 30 minutes | 45 minutes | One hour | 90 minutes | 2 hours or more

‹ Kindle Store

Kindle Short Reads

15 minutes (1-11 pages)

30 minutes (12-21 pages)

45 minutes (22-32 pages)

One hour (33-43 pages)

90 minutes (44-64 pages)

Two hours or more (65-100 pages)

KINDLE SHORT READS: 15 MINUTES

Estimated Number of Pages =1 to 11 pages

Estimated Word Count at maximum 300 words per electronic page =300 to 3,300 words. [Flash fiction and Short Stories]

KINDLE SHORT READS: 30 MINUTES

Estimated Number of Pages =12 to 21 pages

Estimated Word Count at maximum 300 words per electronic page =3,600 to 6,300 words. [Short Stories]

KINDLE SHORT READS: 45 MINUTES

Estimated Number of Pages =22 to 32 pages

Estimated Word Count at maximum 300 words per electronic page =6,600 to 9,600 words. [Novelette]

KINDLE SHORT READS: ONE HOUR

Estimated Number of Pages =33 to 43 pages

Estimated Word Count at maximum 300 words per electronic page =9,900 to 12,900 words. [Novelette]

KINDLE SHORT READS: 90 MINUTES

Estimated Number of Pages =44 to 64 pages

Estimated Word Count at maximum 300 words per electronic page =13,200 to 19,200 words. [Novelette]

KINDLE SHORT READS: TWO HOURS OR MORE

Estimated Number of Pages = 65 to 100 pages

Estimated Word Count at maximum 300 words per electronic page =19,500 to 30,000 words. [Novella]

Longer books above 30,000 words such as short novels are included in the main category charts for that subgenre.

MARKET ANALYSIS OF KINDLE SHORT READS

The Short Reads category has excellent sales across a wide range of subcategories and romance titles dominate, especially at the novella length fiction of around 65 to 100 pages.

For each of the six Short Reads Categories, you can refine your search by category, including LGBT, Literature and Fiction, Romance and Teen and Young Adult, so there is a wide range of opportunities.

For example, for Kindle Store. Kindle Short Reads. Two hours or more (65-100 pages), fiction categories include:

Comics & Graphic Novels

LGBT

Literature & Fiction

Mystery, Thriller & Suspense

Religion & Spirituality [mostly non-fiction]

Romance

Science Fiction & Fantasy

Teen & Young Adult

Here is a quick summary of the level of competition in one of those categories: the Romance category in Short Reads in the Amazon.com Kindle store as a time of writing, April 2023.

Results for your local Kindle Store and time period will be different.

Reading Time	Number of Romance category titles listed of that length
15 minutes (1-11 pages)	More than 6,000
30 minutes (12-21 pages)	More than 10,000
45 minutes (22-32 pages)	More than 10,000
One hour (33-43 pages)	More than 10,000
90 minutes (44-64 pages)	More than 30,000
Two hours or more (65-100 pages)	More than 50,000

So, there is lots of competition! But don't forget the other categories where you could place your short fiction.

My recommendation?

Take the time to research the books which are being sold in these Amazon Short Read categories. Are they a good fit for the length of book you want to write and the niche you want to write in? Research the other niche categories where these books have been classified.

Can you find books in these niches which you would want to read, or have already read?

Look at the cover designs and book titles and subtitles. Are there some common themes? What would make you want to buy that book? Could you image yourself writing and promoting those books?

You will notice that short reads are normally priced from 99 cents, which is the minimum for the Kindle store, on which you can expect a 35% Royalty.

This is entirely reasonable considering the word count, but it is also an attractive price which encourages readers to purchase more eBooks. Hence the number of series of linked short reads in each category.

Let's take a close look at books ranked #3 and #4 on this Two-Hour Romance Short Reads Chart.

Are We Flirting or Nah? By J.D. Light. 69 pages.

Amazon Best Sellers Rank: #743 Paid in Kindle Store

#1 in Two-Hour LGBT Short Reads

#6 in Gay Romance

#3 in Two-Hour Romance Short Reads

Instant Obsession by C.M. Steele. 75 pages.

Amazon Best Sellers Rank: #768 Paid in Kindle Store

#70 in New Adult & College Romance (Books)

#135 in Contemporary Romance (Kindle Store)

#4 in Two-Hour Romance Short Reads

A bestseller sales rank of 500 to 1000 is equivalent to 175 to 113 downloads per day, and daily sales of approx. $40 to $60 at 99cents list price and 35% Royalties. This is therefore an attractive option for books between 50 to 100 pages in length.

The good news is that when you publish your book on KDP, you select the two main categories which are the best fit for your book, then Amazon **automatically assigns it to one of the six Short Reads collections depending on the number of virtual pages in your manuscript and your main categories.**

You don't select Short Reads. Amazon does it for you.

5. What are Romance Tropes?

ROMANCE THEMES

Have you ever wondered why so many short romance titles have words such as: "Billionaire", "Stepbrother", "Bridesmaid", "Wedding" or "Boss" in them?

Those word are part of the promise to a reader that this book will have a certain type of story with a familiar plot or character theme.

A "Trope" can broadly be defined as a plot theme which a reader can recognise. Essentially it is a shortcut word or term which tells a reader precisely what kind of book they should expect to find.

Amazon wants readers to find the precise kind of romance that they are looking for – fast.

This is why they provide a checklist of popular themes readers can use to sort through their subcategory. This list is bound to change and shift according to popularity and your chosen subcategory. A Beaches theme may not apply to a Paranormal listing, for example.

Other tropes such as brother's best friend, reverse harem and single dad are worth looking out for in your search.

Amazon also has another Search Feature –Romantic Heroes.

The good news is that you, as the author, are the one who decides when you come to publish your book:

*Which two main categories and/or niche subcategory are the best fit for your romance.

*The seven Keywords and/or Keyword Strings which will help readers to discover your work – including **the romantic theme** and **type of romantic hero** which best describe your story.

KDP provided a guide on the kind of keywords you should use on Amazon.com here>>
https://kdp.amazon.com/en_US/help/topic/G201216130

TELL Amazon where you want them to place your book.

Romantic Themes
- [ ] Amnesia
- [ ] Beaches
- [ ] International
- [ ] Love Triangle
- [ ] Medical
- [ ] Second Chances
- [ ] Secret Baby
- [ ] Vacation
- [ ] Wedding
- [ ] Workplace

Romantic Heroes
- [ ] Alpha Males
- [ ] BBW
- [ ] Bikers
- [ ] Cowboys
- [ ] Criminals & Outlaws
- [ ] Doctors
- [ ] Firefighters
- [ ] Highlanders
- [ ] Pirates
- [ ] Royalty & Aristocrats
- [ ] Spies
- [ ] Vikings
- [ ] Wealthy

Amazon will then add your eBook to additional virtual shelves depending on the criteria you have provided and automatically assign it to one of the Short Reads categories.

This combination of main categories and Short Reads categories will give your work the best chance of being discovered by the ideal reader.

PART TWO. CREATIVE WRITING

6. Story Craft

Image Credit: iStockPhoto

> *"Romance isn't about the plot, it's about the characters and how they react in certain situations. It's about individuals."*
>
> *Romance Author Lynne Connelly.*

When you turn the last page of a book, what do you remember most? The thrilling action scenes? The unexpected plot twist that made you gasp?

In my experience, what I remember most about a particular romance story are the characters. Something about the hero made me swoon and fall in love with him just as the heroine did.

And what about that heroine? I wanted that girl to be my best friend. She was the equal of the hero and made him work for her love.

Note. In this part of the book, I refer to the hero and heroine for convenience, but all of these aspects apply equally well to LGBT romance fiction.

THE FIVE KEY ELEMENTS OF ROMANCE FICTION

There are five fundamental elements in every traditional romance novel:

• Two main characters that readers can relate to and want to get together. The heroine, who is usually the female main character, and a hero.

• A central romantic storyline where our two characters fall in love and develop a relationship.

• A series of barriers and struggles that the heroine and hero have to overcome to make the relationship work. These conflicts are both physical and emotional.

• An emotionally satisfying ending which usually results in some kind of emotional commitment.

• At the end of your romance, readers should believe that your hero and heroine have a real adult long term and committed relationship, which will continue after you have turned the final paper, or virtual, page in your short story, novella or short novel.

A satisfying emotional ending to your romance is essential for the readers. They have followed these two characters and walked in their shoes on the roller coaster ride of falling in love. Now they want to see them being loved for who they truly are, by someone who has won their trust and love. That is the basis for any long-standing relationship.

WHY IS IT SO IMPORTANT TO HAVE A HAPPY ENDING?

Romance fiction is a literature of hope and optimism.

That is why the clear majority of romance fiction has a happy ending or what is known as a "HEA," which is an abbreviated form of "and they lived happily-ever-after" which was a classic ending for traditional European fairy stories for children.

The reader, who is usually female, wants to be reassured that they can find and enjoy a happy romantic relationship with a partner who values and loves them for who they truly are as an individual.

Your job as a writer is to make the reader fall in love with the hero and heroine at the same time as the characters on the page, so that the reader experiences the vicarious thrill of that romance.

These two characters have found the great love of their lives. The one person in the world, who understands them completely and loves them despite of their faults and failings.

The greater the challenges to this romance, the more satisfying the ending when the lovers conquer these barriers that separate them and take a leap of faith in their love to stay together.

That is what keeps readers hooked into your romance from start to end. When they close your story, you want your reader to sigh with delight and satisfaction that these two people who were meant to be together have found long lasting love.

WHY YOU NEED THREE DIMENSIONAL CHARACTERS FOR YOUR ROMANCE FICTION

Have you ever read a piece of fiction and were so incensed by the characters and their actions that you felt like throwing the book at the wall? Or deleting it from your eBook reader at that instant?

I have. I read a romantic suspense novel last year that annoyed me so much that I actually gave the book away. This author used to be one of my favourites and I adored two of his previous novels.

Why did I feel so annoyed and disappointed?

Simple. I did not believe or sympathise with any of the main characters.

The readers of romance fiction want to walk with the main characters – usually the heroine – and step into their shoes and fall in love at the same time as the characters do.

Think of a wedding scene or a party. You may want to refer quickly to Cousin Frank with the nose stud and piercings or Aunt Phoebe in the pink designer tweed suit, but they do not appear again, and you don't gift them with dialogue.

Focus your character development on the main characters and make them as three dimensional, real and flawed as possible within the context of your story.

WHAT DO WE MEAN BY THREE DIMENSIONAL CHARACTERS?

The three dimensions we are talking about in this context are:

Height. Is this person one of the important main characters in the hierarchy of characters in this story? In short fiction, the cast list must be small.

Breadth. Does this character have quirks and traits and individual attributes which make them distinctive? They should have flaws and weaknesses as well as strengths to make them real and come alive.

Depth. Is this character more than they appear on the surface? As the romance develops, the hidden inner person will emerge under the light of the relationship.

The main protagonists, and antagonists if your story needs them, should have all three dimensions. Don't be afraid to give your characters flaws and weaknesses to balance out their positive attributes.

7. How to Develop Unforgettable Characters

Image credit: iStockPhoto

The best and simplest way to start is with two characters - your hero and your heroine. One world and one-story idea, or situation, which will bring them together.

Note: I am going to refer to the heroine in these questions, but you then replicate all of this for the hero.

Start asking deep and searching questions about how your character sees the world and how it works, and her place in that world.

The answers will determine the type of decisions that she will make during the story and how her world view will shift – or "arc" - from the start to the end of the story because of the romance with the hero.

One thing, however, is crucial to the success of your romance fiction.

The profile you create for your characters must be credible and understandable.

For example. Imagine that you are writing a contemporary romantic comedy novella where your heroine lives in a small mountain town and she specialises in arranging themed weddings. She started the business with her long-standing boyfriend who is an excellent wedding photographer.

When the story opens our heroine arrives at the wedding venue only to find that her boyfriend has just run off with the bride that was due to get married that day, leaving her to clear up the mayhem of the ruined expensive luxury wedding.

Her reluctance to start a new trusting relationship with the best man who has always admired her from afar would be more credible.

The internal barriers that the heroine has created to having any kind of relationship must be there from the start.

Then you can add on the extra barriers to her falling for the hero you are going to drop into her life.

To help you build compelling characters, I would like to share the six-step character development process that I use for my own work.

CHARACTER DEVELOPMENT. STEP ONE

This is the truly fun part of any story development process.

You are completely free to choose any character type or location or story situation you like in any romance subgenre or time frame or story world.

The goal is this; to create a Story Situation frame around your characters and the world they inhabit and then set them free within the confines of that frame.

Start by playing the "what if" game to explore the maximum number of possibilities for the characters and situations.

At the end of Step One of your story development process, you will have a hero and a heroine and a story situation which will both bring them physically together and has the potential to drive them apart.

Example:

Our hero and heroine.

Your hero has been estranged from his father since his mother died in a car crash where his father was driving. He blamed his father and went off and made his fortune on his own and is now a top big city business consultant.

Your heroine is the daughter of the woman the hero's father wants to marry. She admires the hero's father and wants her mother to be happy.

Story situation. The hero's father and the heroine's mother have invested everything they have in their family restaurant and it means everything to them. The business is in trouble and needs to be turned around.

They need the hero to come back and help keep the family business alive.

Where can you take this story? Does it have to be a family restaurant? It could be a luxury hotel in Paris or a steamship on the Mississippi river. Perhaps you are writing western fiction, and this is a large cattle ranch where the only son has to return to take over the ranch. The family dynamics would be just the same.

CHARACTER DEVELOPMENT. STEP TWO

Character Goals and Stakes

What does each of your main characters want when the story opens?

The hero and the heroine must have a powerful and all - consuming short-term goal when the story opens which is easy to understand and for the reader to relate to.

The stakes for reaching that goal must be set high to make the reader care.

Using the example above, what do you think the hero wants when he walks back into the family restaurant after ten years? His mother gave her life to this place and worked tirelessly for no rewards. He wants to close it.

And what do you think the heroine wants at that same moment? She wants to save it for her mother.

What would happen if the characters failed to achieve their goal? Why should we care?

This is a crucial element in creating believable character motivation. How? By making the character sympathetic and empathetic.

CHARACTER DEVELOPMENT. STEP THREE

Develop the external conflicts between the hero and heroine based on the story situation and their individual desires and goals.

The story desire line is the question which will be answered by the end of the story.

Will the hero and heroine be able to work together to save the family restaurant?

How can they fall in love along the way?

CHARACTER DEVELOPMENT. STEP FOUR

Brainstorm the background history of the main characters and focus on the events in the character's past that are still haunting them today. This is their "ghost".

• How has that event or events informed their current controlling and limiting belief systems which set the rules about how they live their life?

• What other weaknesses and flaws does the character have?

• What are their greatest weakness and their greatest fear?

• But also, what is their greatest strength?

This is crucial to developing the internal emotional conflicts which will keep the hero and heroine apart.

When the story opens the character will come on stage with those rules and limiting belief systems all in place.

During the course of the story, these beliefs will be challenged and the damaging and limiting elements overcome with the help of the other romance character – who in turn has their own set of controlling beliefs.

In the opening chapters the reader will only know how the character reacts to the challenges they are hit with, but it is crucial that you know the deep-seated root cause of these beliefs which the foundation for the character's internal conflicts are.

Readers expect that there could be several layers to these beliefs, which will be revealed at the crisis key decision points in the story.

For example, our hero is a loner who never wants to come back to this small town again, so he has cut off any distractions, and deliberately kept friends who have tried to get close to him at arm's length. He does not want to fall in love and go through that pain of loss again.

The only problem? There might come a time when he really needs help and feels lonely and he's not going to have a single person to call.

It's usually true that the external desire will be a selfish want – something the protagonist wants for him or herself, and the inner need will be unselfish - something the protagonist comes to want for other people.

Also, the character will know that s/he wants that outer desire, but probably has very little idea that what she really needs is the inner desire.

This is a useful guideline because it shows character growth over the course of the story through the story events.

Your job as an author is to then create a sequence of steps which clearly show how the character changes and the different kind of decisions that they make, because of the impact of the romance relationship.

CHARACTER DEVELOPMENT. STEP FIVE

Describe the ordinary world of the character when the story opens.

What is their lifestyle? Big city or a small town? Is it contemporary or historical or fantasy? Where do they live and work? What does the setting look and feel like in the opening scene? What time of year is it? Can she smell tropical flowers blowing in on the warm breeze or hear the crunch of crisp snow under her boots?

CHARACTER DEVELOPMENT. STEP SIX

Picture what your characters look like. Use photos of celebrities and actors and actresses if you like as inspiration.

How do they dress? Are they tall, short, slim or round?

Give them names appropriate for the subgenre. Historical characters will be different from paranormal and futuristic. Make the profiles feel real by giving the characters quirks and individual traits.

For example. My restaurant contemporary heroine may like to arrive at work on a motorcycle. Or listen to classical music while she works.

CHARACTER PROFILES

At the end of this section, you should be able to answer all of the following questions:

• Who is the central character you want the reader to empathise with?

This is usually the heroine or the hero in a romance story.

• Why are they at the end of their tether at the start of the story?

• How are they in deep emotional trouble at this point in the story?

• What do they want at that precise moment in the story?

Their short-term IMMEDIATE goal or desire?

• What are the stakes if they do not achieve this goal?

• Who or what is stopping them from achieving this goal?

• Where do we first meet this person? Describe the location.

• Create empathy and sympathy for the central character to help the reader emotionally connect with them. Make them likeable and relatable.

• What are their internal emotional issues or conflicts? What is their true internal desire and longing?

• What are the limiting beliefs that they each carry which governs their reactions and behaviours. These are the beliefs that are going to be challenged by the love interest in this story.

8. Conflict in Romance Fiction

Image credit: iStockPhoto

There is a lot of confusion about the different types of conflict in romance fiction so let's get started with the terminology.

First. Let's be clear that conflict in romance does not involve armed struggle or physical conflict and battle.

Instead the dominant conflict – the real battle – is not between physical forces but between the powerful and deep-seated internal belief systems that the hero and the heroine hold.

EXTERNAL CONFLICT

The External Conflict is the obvious clear and surface level gap between the hero and heroine.

This is the story problem or situation. The reason these two people meet and are forced together in the first place. Logic dictates that this is the kick-off to their relationship, so it has to be right there in the first sequence of scenes.

It sets up the location and the reason why the hero and heroine have every reason to distrust or dislike one another.

For example, the hero and heroine are both called back to the same restaurant. The hero believes that any further investment would be a waste of money and wants to sell it or knock it down and build homes on the land rather than try and rebuild the business for his father. The heroine wants to restore the restaurant back to its former glory for her mother and future father-in-law.

For example in my book "Out of the Blue" the hero Fabio works for the heroine's despised Italian relatives and interrupts her birthday party to deliver some important legal documents from the family.

In the story idea for "The Secret Ingredient," Rob Beresford is the arrogant celebrity chef who fired the heroine years earlier when she refused to do what he told her. Now his brother is in love with her best friend. No escape.

The external conflict or plot creates the pressure where the hero and heroine are trapped in a situation like a closed furnace or crucible, where the pressure and heat inside this crucible will build and build over the story until they are forced to make a leap of faith and break down the old barriers in order to escape.

INTERNAL CONFLICT

This is the term which describes the beliefs that the hero and heroine hold about the world and which come to the surface because of the external conflict.

Without this "internal" emotional conflict there is no story.

You find out what those belief systems are by asking deeper and deeper questions.

For example: why does the heroine REALLY want to save this tired old restaurant which is going to take all her mother's savings to restore and make it safe to work in?

What are the deeper reasons why this building is so important to her? You need to dig deep and find the root cause of this desire. Why is she willing to sacrifice so much to save this one place? Then keep asking why until you get to the truth.

Then do the same for the hero. How do his belief system and rules drive him to want to see the restaurant fail?

Internal conflicts usually grow out of that character's past history and personal background and how that has shaped them and made them who they are when the story opens.

It is important to express the emotional responses of the main characters in writing so that the reader understands why this person is feeling and acting the way that they do. Help the reader to understand the motivation.

This is usually done through the short passages of introspection when you switch from the point of view from the hero to the heroine or vice versa. What are they thinking in that moment? How are they reacting to something that has just happened? In those moments, they will give the reader an insight into what is going on inside their heads.

EMOTIONAL CONFLICT

The resulting effects of the internal conflicts has to be so powerful and integral that they would stop the hero and heroine from being together no matter what circumstances which bring the characters together. If these two people were trapped in an igloo or spaceship without any other external conflicts, their limiting, relationship-blocking belief systems would still prevent them from falling in love.

Ultimately, the characters, their romance and indeed the plot are all driven by the conflict between the emotions and internal beliefs of the hero and heroine.

Just as real-life relationships have ups and downs, so do the heroes and heroines in novels. Readers of romance fiction want to see conflicts played out and resolved and the more challenges the lovers face the greater the satisfaction when they are together in the end.

THE EMOTIONAL CONFLICT THAT COMES FROM THE RELATIONSHIP.

Falling in love with someone opens up all kinds of challenges. The biggest one is probably that the fact that it makes you vulnerable.

Top Tip. When the hero and the heroine reveal the reasons WHY they think and behave the way they do and the reason for their limiting belief systems, then they are making themselves totally vulnerable and this moment should be used as a key part of the romance journey.

Opening up about their personal painful past is not easy for either of them since it takes away a piece of armour they have been using to hide the truth. Use that scene or scenes to bring the hero and heroine closer together, strengthening their bond and love for one another.

Sex is the ultimate display of vulnerability. Use the sex scenes or intimate love scenes to strip away the outer veneer from your characters and show how much the character has changed to be able to get to this point where they will trust another human being with their body.

After a sex or intimate scene, everything is different.

HOW CAN YOU CREATE A SATISFYING EMOTIONAL CONFLICT?

By asking questions about the characters and how they are going to change through the story. You might have to do this several times as you find out more and more about your characters.

Aim? To create a character profile for your heroine – then do the same again for your hero. You will have to dig deep to get to the hidden inner turmoil within your heroine.

Then create a sequence of steps which describe how the character changes over the course of the romance.

Readers want to read how your characters are going to have to struggle against some external events or obstacles which form the plot and overcome all of the barriers and internal beliefs so that they can be vulnerable to the other person.

The EMOTIONAL choices the characters make under the pressure of the crucible you have put them into as the author, are a reflection of the controlling belief systems of the hero and heroine.

Your job is to create a series of challenges which will force these belief systems to change as the characters are transformed because of the romantic relationship.

Layer your conflict with highs and lows, advancements and retreats, passion and withdrawal.

Happy light-hearted moments and deep emotional revelations.

Manipulate the sequence of revelations and action and reaction steps in the story so that the reader must keep turning the pages to find out what happens next. The emotional structure sets the pace for the story.

SUMMARY

Here are some suggestions for the type of questions you could ask your main characters as you develop your story.

Let's start with the heroine. Then repeat the whole process with the hero.

• What does the heroine look like to the outside world at the start of this book?

This is the outer shell and public façade that she shows to the world – her public persona and appearance, which will be stripped away as she changes to reveal the real person beneath the outer shell.

• What has she always been afraid of? Her deepest childhood fears.

• Does this character have extra layers of fear in her life when the story begins? For example. Does she fear the power of love and what it can do? Does she fear loss?

• What is their ghost or wound which still causes them pain? What happened in the past that is causing them problems in the present?

• What has she always wanted to do but never been brave enough to go for?

• In her opinion at the start - Why would falling for this hero be the very worst thing that could happen to her?

• In the end, why would falling for this hero be the best thing that could happen to her?

That is what real character arc is all about.

9. Dialogue and Point of View

POINT OF VIEW

The point of view is the position from which the story is told.

In short romance fiction, the viewpoint characters are almost always the hero and the heroine. One character per scene.

The key thing to remember is that the only information that the reader has about this story comes from the words on the page. And those words describe the story as seen from the point of view of a specific character.

For example, if you are describing a scene in a romantic suspense novel from the viewpoint of the hero, who is the detective investigating a crime scene where a coffee shop was set on fire in a suspected arson attack, he will see the same scene differently from the heroine who runs that coffee shop, who has just lost her home and her business.

Each of the characters will have their own worldview and belief systems and internal conflicts and this will influence and bias how they see a situation.

HOW TO USE POINT OF VIEW

Most romance fiction authors use two types of point of view:

FIRST PERSON

The entire story is told from the viewpoint of one person in their own words. This can create a powerful connection between the reader and the mind of the character, but it does limit the amount of action that can be revealed, and the author will have to use advanced dialogue techniques to make sure that the reader is kept informed about what their love interest is feeling. First person short stories can be very effective since the reader is instantly drawn inside the head of the main character. First person POV can work very well for flash fiction and short stories.

THIRD PERSON POV

The writer acts as a narrator and reports on the thoughts and feelings of all the characters. In this way, the reader knows how both the hero and the heroine feel and think about what is happening in the story. The motivations and reactions of the character then become a lot clearer.

It is good practice to give at least one scene to one character and then allow the other character to respond to what has happened so that the reader can get inside the minds of both hero and heroine.

CLOSE THIRD PERSON POV

This is where you go deep inside the head of one character at a time and let the reader understand the deep internal motivation and belief systems that underpin how and why this character is responding during the romance and what they say and do. It tells the story in that character's unique voice.

Then switch to the other character and do the same.

Top Tip. The first scene in your work, at the start of chapter one, is especially important since this is the scene where you are going to grab the attention of the reader and not let them go.

You can choose the hero or the heroine to kick off your story but be aware that this is the character who the reader is going to root for the most, so make sure that they are well motivated with a clear goal which will carry them through the whole book.

DIALOGUE IN ROMANCE FICTION

The way your characters speak and what they say to one another is a crucial element of romance fiction. This is how you bring your characters to life and reveal who they are and what they want and need.

Too much introspection can slow down the pace of a romance and make the reader skip forward to the part where the hero is interacting with the heroine and sparking off one another through words. This is crucial in short stories where each word must convey an enormous amount of information.

You can use dialogue to:

• Reveal quirks and interesting aspects of the character.

• Indicate their background and education through their choice of vocabulary.

• Reveal information about what they want and need.

• As ammunition. When a character reacts angrily or with passion, they can blurt out something that was meant to stay a secret or something hurtful to the other person.

• As tender and sweet expressions of love.

• As a way of demonstrating the change in that person because of the romance relationship.

The heroine might tell the hero at the start of the story that there was no way that she was ever going to sell him the ranch, so he had better get that idea out of his head straight away. Then in the final scene she gives him the ranch as a gift.

10. Setting and Sensuality

Readers of romance fiction come to romance books looking for the emotional thrill and drama of the roller coaster experience of falling in love.

For most adults that involves a physical relationship which develops with the relationship and the mutual level of trust.

Romance writers use a shorthand metaphor for the level of sexuality in a book by saying how "hot" and "steamy" any romance story is.

Image credit: iStockPhoto

INTIMACY AND SENSUALITY IN ROMANCE FICTION

Because there is such a wide range of sensuality in romance fiction, it is important to be very clear from the start about which subgenre your work will fit into.

The most recent trend is towards hotter books which include intimate and sexually explicit scenes as part of the romance relationship and there is no doubt that steamier romances do sell well. But that does not mean that you have to write them.

You may prefer to focus on the intimacy of sensual moments which are full of sexual tension but do not involve a physical relationship.

PASSION IN ROMANCE FICTION

Unless you are writing erotic fiction, the passionate and intense love scenes between your hero and heroine should develop from the spontaneous and deeply emotional physical attraction which is a natural part of the romance relationship for these two individual people.

Just as in life, the couple should be making love not just having sex. There is a difference.

Some romance books read as though the author has simply added a few random love scenes in the text to titillate and because they think that they should include them.

Wrong. A sex scene must be well motivated and completely in phase with that stage in the romance. Otherwise, it does not add to the romance. It detracts from it.

Think of it this way. All romance fiction is a fantasy of an ideal romantic relationship where two people find a lasting love which is going to carry on beyond the pages of this book.

Your personal fantasy may include jumping in and out of bed with someone without making a deep emotional connection with them – but where is the romance for a reader? Where is the journey to a deeply satisfying love affair which will sweep the reader along with the heroine and hero?

That is why it is crucial to make every sex scene as emotional as possible, no matter how physical, sweaty and erotic the love making.

Sex is an important part of any romance story, whether it is an explicit love making scene or repressed emotional angst. But you have to make it real. And that means working on building the love affair, stage by stage, so that the sex scene becomes the true symbol of the trust that has opened up between the hero and heroine to the point where they are willing to be fully vulnerable in this way.

Use the sex scenes as a means to emotionally connect the hero and heroine in the most powerful way and raise the emotional stakes to a new high.

Your goal should always be to write hot, sweet, tender emotional sex that is unforgettable and real for both the hero and the heroine. Your characters should laugh and talk and have fun and build an emotional bridge between them which neither of them will ever forget.

TOP WRITING TIPS

Go inside each of the character's heads and use their point of view to describe their emotional reaction to the love scene so that the reader can vicariously experience what the character is feeling at that moment.

USE THE POWER OF ALL FIVE SENSES

Taste, touch, smell, sight, and sound are the emotive triggers which you can use to create an emotional response.

Perhaps there is a specific aroma which brings back powerful memories for a character? Or just the touch of a woman's fingertips on the hero's skin is enough for the hero to almost lose control?

SETTING

Setting can also be a powerful tool to help a writer create the perfect combination of sensory effects. Think about the luxurious sensation of freshly laundered satin sheets on naked skin, the aromas and chatter of a bustling city coffee shop and the prickle of hot sand under the soles of your feet on a sunny beach.

When you are writing a love scene, think about where the hero and heroine are at that moment and make it as vivid as possible as a lead up to the moment.

For example. Are they in a luxury hotel room with a Jacuzzi? A snowbound mountain chalet with a rug in front of a roaring fire? Across a desk in an office late at night? Or perhaps a roof garden in a city penthouse?

What can they smell and see and feel and taste and hear at that moment which will heighten the sexual attraction?

Use the power of your imagination to create a love scene which evolves naturally from your characters and then use all five senses to make that scene come alive for your readers.

And finally remember that the hero would not be a hero if he did not use protection. Safe sex is important. Not very romantic – but you must find a way to make it part of the scene but as unobtrusive as you can. Make it fun.

Be true to your characters and the romance and your readers will be swept away.

PART THREE. SELF-EDITING FOR ROMANCE WRITERS

11. Storytelling and Story Structure - Two different things

Image credit: Shutterstock

HOW DO WE TELL STORIES?

Storytelling in its purest spoken form has been around since cavemen sat around a campfire.

Have you ever heard a small child describe something exciting? They cannot wait to get the words out. This happened, then this happened and then this happened and suddenly that happened and... until the end.

The basic structure of storytelling still follows the oral tradition.

A series of Action [something happens] and Reaction [and then something else happens because of that action] steps which track the story from beginning to end.

But that is where the comparison must end, because in commercial fiction writing, we have to make the transition from telling the story in person through the spoken word, to writing down that story and describing and capturing the detail so that it is even more vivid to a reader who we will probably never meet.

Story → Writer → Reader

The reader has a one-to-one relationship with the characters you create through the words on the page. The writer is, therefore, the medium of that communication so it is our job to shape the story into a form that is a satisfying reading experience.

It is crucial that you understand that the success of your romance fiction depends on your ability to shape and mould your story into the best and most compelling form possible.

So many writers have excellent ideas for stories, but they don't come to life on the page. You can visualise in your mind the scene when the couple meet for the first time, what they look like, what they say and do and what happens next to pull them apart until they can be together again.

The storyteller in you creates the internal and external world of that story idea.

The best way to make sure that your story and the emotional journey of your hero and heroine are both compelling and irresistible to readers is to use story structure and story craft techniques.

Think of it this way. The basic story is like a solid lump of fine marble which you have cut out from the rock face.

The writer's role is to carve out the story which they know is trapped inside and polish it until it is as clear as possible.

Why is this so important? Because modern readers expect to be entertained. There are certain storytelling conventions which have become engrained into our minds through every book that we have ever read, and every play, radio drama, TV show or movie that we have ever seen, from animated cartoons to the latest special effect blockbuster.

You may not even be aware of these subconscious expectations because they are totally enmeshed in our brains, but as readers we expect the story to be developed in a certain pattern and sequence of events and revelations and stages.

That is why we need Story Craft and, in particular, Story Structure.

Every block of stone has a statue inside it and it is the task of the sculptor to discover it. Michelangelo

WHEN DO YOU NEED STORY STRUCTURE?

When you are developing a story idea and you need to focus on the main theme or opening event, and again when you are revising and polishing your final manuscript.

You might have a specific idea for a hero or heroine and the conflict between them which will drive the story forwards.

Or perhaps there is a specific setting or opening scene which you can see vividly in your mind?

This is where story structure helps you to explore and expand that idea into a form which readers can enjoy.

For example: Perhaps the hero and heroine were once lovers and they meet up again at the wedding of a friend they both knew at university.

What will bring these two characters together in a way that locks them together in the course of your story? How have they changed and what belief systems have they created which will act as barriers to any romance?

List out all of the possible situations that you can think of, where the mistaken attitudes and beliefs that these two characters have will come into direct conflict as that they fall in love. Make them suffer!

What if the hero is a soldier returning home from active service and is wounded and recovering from the trauma and meets the girl he left behind? The internal conflict of the hero could drive the emotional dynamics of that story.

But every writer is unique, so how does story structure work in practice?

Writers are usually divided into two types, according to the process that they use when they develop their stories.

PLOTTERS.

Some romance writers use the principles of story structure to help shape the story when they are developing it. These are writers who prefer to outline and plot their romance fiction to some extent before they start to write.

Plotters will spend a lot of preparation time building profiles of the main characters and working on their individual quirks and goals and needs before they start writing.

The plotters among us tend to brainstorm a few scenes which will challenge the hero and heroine and have them work together to bring about change through forming a relationship of some sort.

This outline is a very high level overview of the whole story, with perhaps a few lines of dialogue in a brief outline of the plot and the emotional journey the hero and heroine will take, which can then be broken down into sequences of scenes and expanded into text.

PANTSERS.

Other writers prefer to write down the story as it comes to them, often without a clear idea of where the story will go, as though they were "Writing into the mist."

They are writing by instinct. By the seat of their pants.

Once these intuitive writers have a complete first draft of the whole work, they then revise the manuscript so that the story is in the best shape possible. This can mean cutting out a lot of work and replacing scenes with fresh ones.

These writers admit that structure freezes them, and they are prepared to do the extra work of significant rewriting and revision.

Unlike plotters, pantsers may need to write the whole book to discover the twists and turns of the romance relationship for their characters.

Many authors who write this way have a powerful internal sense of story structure which means that they may write the major scenes where the hero and heroine make themselves vulnerable, totally intuitively.

The key to remember is that it does not matter whether you are a plotter or pantser by nature when it comes to developing your story.

Both methods are perfectly fine.

Your process is your process and you must respect that.

Most romance fiction authors, including myself, operate somewhere in the middle and like to have a short outline of the story and the main dynamics in place, before they start writing, but leave plenty of opportunities for this story to change and evolve as the writing progresses.

All the reader cares about is the emotional experience that you have created for them on the page.

Either way, no matter how you come to it, you are going to end up with a rough draft of your manuscript in an outline or more worked form, but a working draft all the same.

Now is the time to start working on the story structure of that working draft so that you can take your hero and heroine on an emotional roller coaster up and down journey to love, which demonstrates the full potential of your characters and the story situation that you have created.

I saw the angel in the marble and carved until I set him free. Michelangelo

IMAGINE THAT YOU ARE BUILDING A HOUSE.

Stage One. The foundations are going in. Concrete and services.

Stage Two. You are going to need walls, floors, and ceilings.

Stage Three. Is the interior and exterior design. The surface gloss and sparkle. Paint colours, soft furnishings and wall hangings to make the home look as polished and attractive as possible.

For short fiction, we have to start with a rock-solid foundation which will hold our house up where there is little space for interior design.

You have your story idea or story situation. You have created profiles for both your hero and heroine and understand their external and internal conflicts - but you know that you will find out a lot more when you get them together.

Now you need a form which will tell this story in the most effective way.

This means that your first draft of the novel needs to have a number of key dramatic twists or reveals, called "turning points", when the story shifts or something is revealed and the stakes increase. In this way, the story moves on and builds, and there are no sagging middles but a controlled pace.

The best analysis of story structure comes from screenwriters. Their job is to choreograph and control the emotions of the audience who is watching the movie at every minute.

THE FIVE KEY TURNING POINTS IN ALL ROMANCE FICTION

Whether your work is 4,000 words or 40,000 words, there are six major stages, made up of sequences of scenes with five turning points where new decisions have to be made and the story spins off in a new direction.

This is how the wonderful screenwriter and writing coach Michael Hague describes it.
[http://storymastery.com/articles/30-screenplay-structure]

Michael Hauge's
Six Stage Plot Structure

0%	10%	25%	50%	75%	90-99%	100%
Stage I: SETUP	Stage II: NEW SITUATION	Stage III: PROGRESS	Stage IV: COMPLICATIONS & HIGHER STAKES		Stage V: FINAL PUSH	Stage VI: AFTERMATH
Turning Point #1: Opportunity		Turning Point #2: Change of Plans	Turning Point #3: Point of No Return	Turning Point #4: Major Setback	Turning Point #5: Climax	
Act I			Act II		Act III	

Important – The Percentage figures for the Acts do NOT equate to word count in a novel. They are guidelines for screenplays.

You do NOT divide your book into four and write exactly one quarter of the total word count for each of the four acts.

It COULD be done that way, but in my experience the further you go along in your novel, the more compressed each sequence of scenes can become.

As you rush towards the end of your story the events escalate furiously, the tension is rising, and things have snowballed into bigger and bigger stakes and the relationship is in crisis.

But the five turning point technique is still a useful tool to structure a loose collection of words and pages into a form which makes sure that the hero and heroine must undergo a real journey before they can be together.

The turning points set way markers and milestones on that journey your characters are taking.

Most importantly, the six-scene sequence structure makes sure that your story will meet the expectations of your readers who want to see the characters battle against the odds and make the wrong choices before they can be together.

12. What is Emotional Story Structure?

ANY ROMANCE STORY IS MADE UP OF FOUR INTERWOVEN STORY TRACKS.

THE CENTRAL DESIRE LINE OR THE GOAL OF THE MAIN CHARACTER IN THE STORY.

This is the central spine of the book on which everything else hangs. The story structure locks the central desire line as the firm support for everything else. The external conflict feeds this line and spins out from it.

THE HEROINE'S CHARACTER ARC.

The inner emotional journey and character arc that the heroine goes through. How she is transformed by the romance relationship over the course of your story.

THE HERO'S CHARACTER ARC.

The inner emotional journey and character arc that the hero goes through. How he is transformed by the romance relationship just as the heroine is.

But at the heart of any romance fiction is

THE ROMANCE STORY TRACK.

The steps that the hero and heroine will take to find love.

The romance storyline are the rungs of a ladder which lock the character arc of the hero with the character arc of the heroine as the story progresses, pulling them closer together as they fall in love.

Each of the characters changes when they fall in love. They are moulded and shaped because of the intense heat of the attraction and love affair inside the crucible that we as authors have created for the hero and the heroine. They must face new situations and make difficult choices which will define their future.

Because the romance and character arc strands are locked onto the central goal line of the story, you can build up a series of unique story events that will make your romance fiction absolutely individual.

The balance between these four story tracks will be determined by the kind of story that you are telling.

In romantic suspense, the central desire line will dominate since the goal of the main character is to discover who carried out the crime or escape the threat. So perhaps 70% goal driven storyline and 30% romance and character arc.

In a modern contemporary category romance, this will be reversed and perhaps 10% goal driven storyline and 90% romance and character arc.

But all four story strands will be there.

HOW TO USE STORY STRUCTURE

The challenge with all short fiction is that you have to include all of the elements of the four-track emotional journey that the characters will go on, but don't have many scenes to achieve that.

There are three key things to remember:

#1. The romance story and the two main characters come first. There simply is no room for secondary plots and a large cast list. That is why it is crucial that you have invested time in developing compelling characters that will leap out from the page from the very first paragraph.

#2. You need to combine emotional and classical story structure to create a deeply satisfying romance story that is complete and rich and hits all five turning points – even if it is only one large extended scene.

#3. It does not matter if you are a pantser who prefers to use story structure at the revision stage, or a plotter who uses structure to help you to create an outline for their story before you start. Both approaches are valid.

13. Story Structure for the Short Novel and Novella

Imagine that you are writing a short novel which is made up of 12 chapters. I would suggest that the first three chapters of any romance fiction novel form the crucial Stage One of the book.

SEQUENCE ONE.

This is setting up the ordinary world of your hero and heroine.

At some point in Chapter One, something happened to interrupt the normal world of the main character. There is a sudden change or new opportunity or challenge which must addressed. [Turning Point One]

SEQUENCE TWO.

Chapters 2 and 3 then have the characters evaluating this challenge until they come to a decision at the end of Chapter 3 which will make them commit to some initiative or working together on a new adventure in their lives with a new goal. This sets the story question. Will this character achieve their new goal by the end of this story? [Turning Point Two]

SEQUENCE THREE.

The characters leave the ordinary world behind and start work on the new goal.

Chapters 4 to 6 are the falling in love scenes which end at the Critical Midpoint of No Return where there is some form of personal commitment [the sex or intimacy at 60 in a 120-page screenplay].

SEQUENCE FOUR

Chapters 7 to 9 are the complications where the love has changed their worlds and the stakes are increased. Leading to a Crisis Decision which is [Turning Point Four].

SEQUENCE FIVE

Chapter 10 is the battle to save their relationship leading to a climax scene when everything is at stake and desperate decisions must be made. This is the black moment when the relationship is in peril. Someone must take a leap of faith and compromise or negotiate because this relationship is worth the sacrifice. [Turning Point Five].

SEQUENCE SIX

Followed by the resolution / aftermath in Chapters 11 and any Epilogue to show the new life as a couple.

For a short story or novella, the word count for each sequence of scenes is going to be a lot shorter than in a novel and many authors choose to combine stages one and two so that they move as quickly as possible into stage three and the sequence of scenes which describes the characters falling in love.

In a short novel, you may have longer scenes and more time to explore setting and sensual detail so that the reader has a richer experience.

14. Story Structure for The Short Story

SHORT STORIES

With a maximum of 7,000 words to work, here are a few top tips on how you can build an effective short story. All of the story structure elements discussed in the previous chapter must be there – but compressed and refined to create an exhilarating emotional experience for a reader in a few pages.

Introduce your main character and immediately and show how they are at the end of their tether and how they are facing a real problem which has high stakes.

The goal is to engage the reader and connect them to this character - fast!

This means that you have to shamelessly hook the reader by making them sympathise and empathise with the main character – usually the heroine – as soon as possible. The first few paragraphs are crucial!

The love interest must be on the page as soon as possible and definitely by the end of the first turning point.

The reader wants to see how the hero and heroine are going to act and react to the layers of conflict that they are going to have to overcome before they can have a real romance relationship. T

his is one of the reasons why many romance authors prefer the characters to have met before at some point. They can then use that memorable previous relationship, good or bad, as a short-cut to the romance.

Make the first turning point into something powerful and emotional so that the reader feels that these two characters have made a decision or commitment which is true to who they are.

The romance must build until the midpoint of no return where they are bound together in a way that means that they face the challenges in the next scene which will usually make the problem worse.

Then at the climax of the story the main character takes a leap of faith of some sort, encouraged by the romance relationship, and wins the day.

You want your readers to be totally engrossed in this short romance so don't be afraid to make it as powerful and passionate or emotive as you can.

15. Editing for Romance Writers

One of the things they don't tell you when you sign the contract with a traditional publishing house is that the editor who loves your story proposal and your voice is going to read your finished manuscript which you have slaved over for months, and then tell you all of the things that need to be revised before they agree to publish it. And pay you.

REVISIONS?

Expect to rewrite major sections of your book several times.

Sometimes I have had to rewrite whole chapters and update a complete storyline or character arc.

COPY EDITING.

Next there is Copy editing: "the process of reviewing and correcting written material to improve accuracy, readability, and fitness for its purpose, and to ensure that it is free of error, omission, inconsistency, and repetition."
https://en.wikipedia.org/wiki/Copy_editing

Copy editors check overarching grammatical structure, layout, punctuation and references.

PROOFREADING.

It is amazing how an independent person can spot spelling and punctuation errors and mistakes that you cannot believe you missed.

Your goal is to deliver excellent quality so that any reader who purchases your book knows and expects that they will not be disappointed by spelling mistakes or pulled out of the story because a character is called one name at the beginning of the story and another name at the end.

After 19 novels I can share with you the fundamental truth.

The book that your readers will buy is a more compelling story because of the editing and revisions. No doubt about it.

But what happens when you don't have the services of a traditional publisher?

THE QUALITY OF THE WRITING AND THE FORMAT

The challenge is that many romance eBooks are often self-published online without proofreading, copyediting or the correct formatting for that digital platform.

This has created an expectation in many readers that self-published books are often badly written, and it is better if they stay with authors they are familiar with.

How do you stand out in the crowded fiction market?

By investing the time to understand and apply story craft to create a satisfying emotional experience for your readers.

Then we might just have a chance of finding the readers who would love our stories.

EDITING IS A KEY PART OF PUBLISHING ANY BOOK.

It can be very difficult to be objective with our own work, but you should have meticulously revised the text to make sure that:

• There is a single clear external plot line, or desire line, which forms the backbone of your story.

At the beginning of your story, and certainly by the end of Act One, the reader should be able to ask a central story question which will be answered by the end of the book. For example, will the female detective find the serial killer? Who are the hero and heroine, and will they be reunited and find happiness, despite all of the barriers between them?

• Setting. Think of the sensory detail linked to the location of the novel. An old house smells and creaks differently from a new apartment. The light in a beach cottage will be very different from a mountain cabin. What do your characters eat and drink? In a rush from plastic containers or in fine restaurants which specialise in a certain type of cuisine? The reader should be able to smell and taste every mouthful, from cheeseburger to fine red wine.

• Everything starts with the characters and the story idea, so for me it is essential to work on Story Editing and be happy with a final draft of the manuscript before moving onto the copy edits and proofreading.

• There is a clear character arc for each of the main characters. A reader is looking for someone who they can root for and step into their shoes for the length of this novel. Have you shown that your main character is at the end of their tether at the start of the book, and how are they different at the end, because of the decisions that they have had to take because of the romance?

All of the secondary characters and subplots have been resolved before the conclusion of the main plot and these subplots have been woven skilfully into the central storyline.

There are many romance authors who go through four or five revisions cycles, adding emotional depth, sensory detail and ruthlessly making sure that the dialogue and settings are as effective as they can be in their manuscripts.

So should you.

GENERAL ROMANCE STORY STRUCTURE

There are four overarching components of any piece of romance fiction, irrespective of the length.

• The Main A Romance Story. How the romance relationship builds.

• B Plot. The Character Arc of the Heroine over the course of the story.

• C Plot. The Character Arc of the Hero over the course of the story.

• D Plot. The external story situation which will bring the hero and heroine together, even if they are battling against one another for the same prize. In most cases this acts as the spine for the story.

Use the same process to track the storylines from start to end.

STEP ONE. CREATE A WORKING OUTLINE OF YOUR ENTIRE STORY

The first thing I will do is to print out the complete manuscript and read through every chapter and write down the sequence of steps that takes the reader on an interesting journey from start to finish.

I have no problem scribbling all over my pages in red or green pen, striking through or correcting text, and adding sticky notes for changes.

This is the spine of the book and the book ends when the external conflict is resolved, and the hero and heroine can start a real relationship.

Because this is a short book [target 40,000 words] the pacing must be kept brisk. No hanging around talking for two chapters.

My Process? Create an outline of the steps from chapter one to the end.

*What happens when the scene opens?

*What happens next? An Action or Reveal followed by an Emotional and Physical Reaction.

*What happens next? Action or Reveal followed by an Emotional and Physical Reaction.

*What happens next? Action or Reveal followed by an Emotional and Physical Reaction.

...and so on. To create a series of clues, actions, reveals and reactions.

• Does every scene move the story forwards or reveal something? Is there conflict of some sort in every scene?

• Does the story make sense? Or do I need to add another scene and/or rewrite a flat one?

• Can I cut and streamline to increase the pace without losing content? Do I really need that long introspection?

The goal is to provide an emotional experience that satisfies readers, not great sections of exposition showing off all of the research that I have carried out on luxury yachts in the South of France/Florida/

STEP TWO. CHARACTER ARCS FOR BOTH THE HERO AND THE HEROINE.

At the end of the story, does the reader see how the hero and heroine have changed from the characters they were at the start the book as a result of the romance relationship?

Character change = interest and engagement.

Can I use symbolism to demonstrate the change from the first pages to the last?

THE CHARACTER ARC FOR THE HEROINE

• What is her short-term goal when the story starts – a simple external goal with a clear endpoint and preferably linked to a chance to achieve her longing or need – she has to do this to make a big change in her life? This could be as simple as making it back in time for her birthday party.

• What are the stakes? What happens is she does not achieve this goal?

• Why now?

• What is her long-term goal – her longing- that deeply held desire which she has not found the courage to go after yet?

• What is her need? The thing that is missing in her life which will make it complete?

• What is her wound – the un-healing source of continuing pain? This has led to the identity mask that they show to the world – which will be chipped away during the story journey.

• What is the one overpowering dilemma in this story? And who does it belong to? The dilemma is the choice between staying in the past or moving forward and taking the risk – and it belongs to the person who changes most.

THE CHARACTER ARC FOR THE HERO

You then ask precisely the same questions of your hero?

Can the reader see how the romance has helped the hero to overcome his limiting beliefs?

Have you introduced the hero as a potential romantic interest in a subtle and believable way? Have I show her reaction to him and made him come alive through dialogue and actions?

In a short novel you have space to introduce a subplot with at least two or three secondary characters who will be coming back in other books as supporting cast, who all live in this community.

They must have quirks and mannerisms and feel real. Have I shown them chatting and interacting and adding balancing humor?

In a novella you would be pushing to have more than one or two continuity characters.

STEP THREE. THE EXTERNAL CONFLICT/STORY IDEA MUST BE RESOLVED

An external conflict or story situation brought the hero and heroine together at the start of the story.

Can you show in the final scenes that this conflict has been resolved as a direct result of the romance relationship?

That initial conflict acted like a hook and raised a question in the mind of the reader. Don't short-change them by not answering the question that sparked this romance.

STEP FOUR. GENERAL FICTION EDITING

I want this to be a fast-paced, short read, so there is not a lot of space for filler backstory or exposition.

Setting. Have I created a sense of place for my fictional setting through careful use of a few specific details? What time of year is it? Where does my romance couple live and work etc.?

Use details to make the setting come alive – this is why historical and paranormal romance are so very popular. Readers love to dive into wonderful new worlds and have a visceral experience through the eyes of the characters.

Point of View, Dialogue and Dialogue tags. I like close third person point of view, so I can use introspection as part of the character's reaction to events and revelations. This does create a challenge for speech tags.

Characterization. Focus on a few key aspects and let the dialogue and reaction from other characters fill in the gaps.

STEP FIVE. LINE EDITS AND PROOFREADING, INCLUDING FORMATTING.

Don't let the reader be pulled out of the story by spelling errors, or major formatting problems.

If you changed the name of the hero from draft one to draft two, it is your role as the publisher to make sure that the old name has not crept back in again. Same with repeated snatches of dialogue and description.

Grammar and punctuation are important to the reading experience. If you are stuck, try using the free version of the Grammarly or ProWritingAid software tools to give your work the final polish.

STEP SIX. BETA-READERS

If you have the time and the opportunity, send the final manuscript to an editor who is a specialist in this genre, or beta-readers and friends for them to read on condition that they are going to be ruthless in their feedback.

After 19 novels I can share with you the fundamental truth. The book that your readers will buy is a more compelling romance story because of the editing and revisions. No doubt about it.

PART FOUR. BUILDING AN EBOOK

16. The Practical Aspects of Building an eBook

Image Credit: iStockPhoto

LAYOUT

A short romance fiction book is made up of three parts:

#1. Front Matter: The Table of Contents, a Book Description and possibly an invitation to subscribe to an author's newsletter.

#2. Body of the Book: Formatted text.

#3. The Back Matter. The final pages of the book. This would normally include:

• A list of any other books you have written and links to your author page.

• Your biography and official author photo. Links to your website and social media platform.

• The copyright page.

The copyright page should have all the publishing information about the book. Including:

• The publisher's name and contact details if you have decided to create your own publisher brand for your books.

• The date of publication and the publishing history such as editions and formats.

• The copyright line. This is given as the copyright symbol, followed by the copyright holder's name and the year of first publication. For example. ©NinaHarrington.2020

• The copyright notice and assertion of rights.

• A disclaimer for fiction authors that the characters and storyline is completely imaginary.

• Credit to the cover designer or the stock photo library that was used to create the cover artwork. (Optional)

You do not need an ISBN for a Kindle eBook.

Amazon gives each eBook a 10-digit ASIN (Amazon Standard Identification Number), which is unique to the eBook, and is an identification number for the Kindle Book on Amazon.

In print books the copyright page is in the front matter but for eBooks it is usually moved to the back of the book.

Why? Because the opening pages of eBooks can be sampled online and downloaded as an extract in the '*Look Inside*' feature.

Authors want readers to enjoy the text of the book and not have to read through a page of copyrights notices.

Using the back and front pages as a promotional tool

> *"The moment after someone finishes your book is the point when they are most favorably inclined to you as an author."* <u>Courtney Milan</u>

• Thank the reader and invite them to sign up for the new releases newsletter at your website or to subscribe to your blog.

• Then ask them to post an honest review. Make it easy by sharing the link to the online bookstores where your book is live.

• The call to action which should be linked to some offer which is of value to your readers. A special gift, like the one which I am offering with this eBook that you are reading now, links to free exclusive book extracts or more bonus content.

• Invite them back to your website to read a free extract from another of your books, a short story or something else that they would find interesting and valuable. And while they are on your website, why not sign up for your updates or more free chapters and stories, or subscribe to your blog?

These are all valid ways to move the reader from Amazon over to your website, where you can ask for their email address in a friendly and useful way without the hard sell.

Note - you can add links to other Kindle books that you have written in the back pages of your Kindle book on the Amazon Kindle Book store, but you must remove those references when loading your book as an ePUB file onto other bookstores like Smashwords, Kobo, iTunes and Nook. In that case, direct the reader straight to your website.

The back page of your book is the ideal opportunity for a self-published author to make a stronger connection with their readers.

Remember – never ask a reader for favours. Always be the one providing valuable content for free.

Clearly this offer will only be attractive if you have created an excellent book and your readers want to know where they can find out more.

Amazon KDP offers authors a full range of technical support articles and information on how to publish your manuscript which is constantly kept up to date with best practices, so I am going to focus on the practical aspects of transforming the text document that is your romance story, into a form which you can submit to KDP.

There is full guidance and support online at Amazon for this part of the process.

The entire publishing plan for your eBook starts with creating a compelling quality manuscript that you can be proud of.

You should be confident that there is no way that you can improve the text, and your romance is as compelling and emotive as it can possibly be.

17. Book Cover Design.

The Cover Art.

A crucial part of any publication is the cover.

There are subtle conventions with every subgenre of romance fiction and readers expect to see cover designs which match not only other covers in the same niche but make a promise about what kind of book they are going to be buying.

If you are writing a series of short fiction books, consider how the cover art will link the continuity together.

Photo Credit: Flickr/Will Hart

The "***fangs of doom***" will certainly strike if the cover art is tacky and appalling. On the flip side of that, I had bought gorgeous looking books which I put aside after a few chapters because they were so poorly written.

Each cover is a reflection of your business. Show the readers that you take pride in your work and that you are a professional author who has invested in a professionally designed cover.

This is particularly important for short fiction where you can produce a manuscript very quickly compared to a full-length novel. Investing time and money in a great cover design is one of the best things you can do to market your book, no matter what genre it fits into.

Your cover art for KDP must have an ideal height / width ratio of at least 1.6, meaning a minimum of 625 pixels on the shortest side and 1000 pixels on the longest side. For best quality, your image should be 2500 pixels on the longest side but be careful that your file is less than 3 Megabytes in size.

HOW TO GRAB THE READER WITH A SUPERB COVER DESIGN

We don't judge a book by its cover? *Oh yes, we do.*

When we browse through the titles on Amazon or other bookseller shelves, what is the first thing we look at?

Romance and other genre fiction readers can take one look at a book cover and instantly recognise all the subtle signs that tell them whether your book is something they will risk their money on –or not.

Online sites will display a small thumbnail image of your book cover, and you only have a few seconds to attract a browser before they move onto the next title on the list.

That is why it is essential that you invest in great cover design for your book. Without a quality cover, readers will not click on your book and read the book description, no matter how much marketing and promotion you do.

Cover design for fiction is a very demanding skill. On one flat image you have to capture subtle aspects of the genre and subgenre of the book, the style of the writing and the entire mood of the novel.

This is a complex combination of graphic design, styling and meticulous use of colour.

Here is the cover of one of my contemporary romance titles for the Harlequin Mills and Boon RIVA and Modern Tempted line called '*My Greek Island Fling*'.

The colour range is all summer blue skies and sandy yellows with fluffy white clouds and pop splashes of pinks. My serif author name font matches the tone of the lower-case tag line at the base, and the pen and ink drawing capture a holiday romance tone.

Cover Art for My Greek Island Fling Copyright © 2020 by Harlequin Enterprises Limited. All rights reserved.

I think it is clear to any reader, from the cover image alone, this is a fun light romance – and this is echoed in the tag line at the bottom.

Now contrast this with the draft cover idea for my cozy mystery, *Murder and Merlot*.

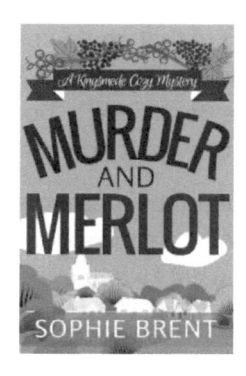

Note the hard, straight vertical lines of the non-serif font used for the title and author name which are all in capitals. The artwork is a high definition stock photo with a bright background colour.

That is why it is crucial that you have collected several examples of book covers from your book genre which you really like, and which would clearly signal to any reader what type of story is inside that book, before they even read the book description.

WHAT ARE YOUR OPTIONS WHEN IT COMES TO COVER DESIGN?

OPTION 1. DESIGN IT YOURSELF

Some writers are able to create an excellent design on their home computer, and there are templates on the internet and on YouTube which describe how to use Microsoft Word, PowerPoint, Canva, Keynote, GIMP, Photoshop or similar graphic design software packages to create a simple cover.

It is worthwhile spending a couple of hours using the search engines of the big stock image catalogues such as Shutterstock and iStockPhoto until you have a few good examples of images that you would love to be on your cover (or use a free trial if you can) and download a test image.

Then add layers and text to that photo image or images using the free software such as Canva.com, which is very easy to use and has templates for Kindle Book covers. Don't buy the image until you have tested it with a cover design and have fun!

I used **Canva.com**, to create the book cover for *Murder and Merlot*. I researched all of the similar books on Amazon and sketched out an idea of what I wanted the cover to do.

• Clearly state that this was a cozy mystery.

• Have Murder in the title since that was the link to the series.

• Be attractive and bright with a large font.

• Show a village scene as the background.

Yes, it did take several days to find an image I liked and experiment with fonts and icons etc. to come up with a design which fitted my genre, but I enjoyed the process and learnt a lot.

This option should only be attempted if you really love colour and design and have a lot of experience with Photoshop or other design software and time to invest.

OPTION 2. PURCHASE A PRE-MADE COVER

Many professional cover design companies and artists have **pre-made** quality covers at reduced prices which could be perfect for your eBook. The range available will be limited to popular subgenres, so you will have to search around to find designs which are a good match for your work. And yes, quality does differ widely.

How to find pre-made covers?

• Search the internet for pre-made romance book covers and make a shortlist.

• Look inside the copyright pages of short fiction you have enjoyed. Most authors should credit the cover designer.

• Well-known cover designers often have pre-made romance options. For example: Killion Publishing, The Book Cover Designer, Rocking Book Covers, The Cover Collection, Bookcoverscre8tive and many more.

One note – think series. Does this designer offer a discount if you buy similar covers in a linked series? Do they have pre-made covers available in series? Many do.

Expect to pay from $50 to $100 for an excellent pre-made eBook cover.

OPTION 3. HIRE A FREELANCE DESIGNER TO CREATE A CUSTOM COVER.

One of the best sources is fiverr where you can hire a freelance from anywhere in the world for five US dollars to design a cover for you. Of course, you should see examples of their work, but you only pay for the work when you are completely happy with it. Many authors commission several designers from fiverr and then select which one gives the best results. Then stick with that designer for complete series and other projects.

Other options are to post a job on freelance designer sites such Upwork.com. Expect to pay from $5 to $50 per design.

OPTION 4. COMMISSION A DESIGN COMPANY

It can pay to commission a professional cover design which is perfect for your work. The designer will need to be briefed on essential information and will usually ask for:

Examples of your favourite book covers in your subgenre. The designer may not understand the subtle differences between a

Regency romance and a contemporary young adult romance and it is your job to help them do that.

The type of image which you want to be on your cover. Don't buy them! The designer will be able to buy the image or a similar one cheaper and then charge you for the licence.

A quick internet search came up with Kim Killion, Damonza, Reedsy, CreativeIndieCovers and 99Designs but there are hundreds of other eBook cover designers with a wide range of prices.

Expect to pay from $150 to $400 for a custom eBook design.

Note – I am only talking about the front cover of an eBook here. If you want to self-publish a print on demand book, then you will also need a spine and back cover design which adds to the cost, but you can find pre-made designs and templates for print books.

This can be useful for short novels, especially if your ideal reader prefers a printed book.

In summary. Don't sabotage your hard work with a poor cover which any romance reader will recognise as DIY and shoddy.

18. Formatting your Manuscript into a Kindle eBook

What makes electronic eBooks different from printed books?

A print book is made up of fixed and fully formatted text.

During any conversion process to an EPUB or Kindle mobi electronic eBook file, your manuscript.doc(x) file will be converted into a "reflowable" responsive eBook format.

This type of file format will automatically adjust the orientation and shape of the contents according to the device your reader is using to read the text, such as tablet, computer or mobile phone, in portrait or landscape mode. Your book will therefore be displayed correctly and fill the screen of the reader's device.

Kindle Direct Publishing (KDP) uses converter software to transform your document into a reflowable Kindle mobi format file which offers the end reader a wide range of custom options.

Kindle eBooks allow the reader to resize text and change the font on all Kindle devices and the free Kindle reading applications.

On the Kindle app on my iPad, for example, I am offered a range of eight fonts: Amazon Ember Bold, Baskerville, Bookerly, Caecilia, Georgia, Helvetica, Open Dyslexic and Palatino. Plus, I have a range of line spacing options to select from and two font size adjustment buttons. **Aa⬇** to reduce the font size, and **Aa⬆** to increase the size of the font. There are also four choices of background page colour.

This level of user customization means that the base coding for the eBook must be as simple and logical as possible.

FORMATTING SOFTWARE

You can buy specialist software such as Vellum, or Scrivener and I know many authors who find them easy to use and have had excellent results.

MANUAL METHOD

The good news is that KDP system means that you don't have to know anything about coding to create a professional looking eBook (and KDP print paperback) which is fully acceptable to the KDP converter programmes.

Kindle online publishing works with several word processing applications, such as Microsoft Word, Apple Pages, together with Open Office Writer, Google Docs and other word processing software that export to the .doc(x) format.

Step One. Final Editing, Spelling Checks and Proofread

Now is the time to go through the final draft of your manuscript in detail before starting formatting.

Spelling mistakes, huge grammar errors and copyediting glitches, such as someone's name changing halfway through a novel, or the same paragraph being repeated several times, distract your reader and spoil their enjoyment of your work.

Even worse, they mark you out as being unprofessional and result in poor reviews.

• Have you had the book edited by someone who can be objective about the text?

• Have you read the final draft of the book out loud to yourself? This can pick up missing words, words that you have repeated several times in the same sentence and incorrect paragraph and chapter break points. It is easy to accidently delete the end of a sentence in error. Now is the time to pick these errors up.

• Have you used the automatic spelling and grammar check programs available in your word processing package?

Take the time to run a last spellcheck and proofread your document. It is so easy to miss a word that has the correct spelling but is the wrong word for that context. I know because I have done this myself many times, and I still see it in traditionally published books.

Only move onto the formatting stage when you are completely happy that you cannot improve your document further and you are totally happy to share your work with readers.

Step Two. Remove all formatting

The first part of preparing your manuscript to be published as a Kindle eBook is one of the hardest. You know all those lovely decorative fonts, coloured text and paragraph styles which you used to make your text look appealing?

Sorry. *This is going to hurt*. They must go.

The KDP system will automatically convert your text document into one long continuous piece of computer code when it creates the Kindle mobi file. It will strip out all the unwanted formatting in order to keep the code as clean and simple as possible. This includes font families, pages numbers and headings and footers.

That's why you have to tell the system where the new chapter page breaks are and what styles you want to apply to specific parts of your document such as chapter headings and body text, before you upload your file.

The eBook editing software will then use your styles to create a stylesheet for your electronic document to make sure that all the styles are consistent for the reader.

Yes, I know that this is a completely different way of looking at your manuscript, but hopefully you can now see that eBooks are fundamentally strings of computer code and the cleaner and simpler you can make your manuscript before you upload it onto KDP, the easier it will be to convert the text into a stunning electronic eBook which will be easy for your readers to enjoy.

All eBooks also go through an Amazon review process to ensure that the formatting and content meets the KDP quality standards.

The stylesheet for your electronic book file works using general simple styles instead of the formatting you used when you created your text document.

The simplest and fastest thing to do is to get back to the basic text, which means stripping out ALL the formatting in the entire document.

That will ensure that you are not working with a document in which you have used more than one style or font for the same kind of text in different parts of the book.

Create a new copy of your master text document to work on as your electronic book file.

For Word. Open your document. Press Ctrl +A to select the entire document. Click the *Clear all formatting* button in the Font header menu to remove all formatting. This is the A symbol with the eraser icon.

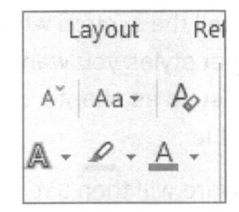

For Google Docs, press Ctrl +A to select the whole document, then go to Format and select *Clear formatting*.

Insert	Format Tools Add-ons	Help	Las
0% ▾	Text	▸	1
1	Paragraph styles	▸	
	Align & indent	▸	
	≣ Line spacing	▸	
	≣≣ Columns	▸	
	Bullets & numbering	▸	
	Headers & footers…		
	Table	▸	
	Image	▸	
	✗ Clear formatting	Ctrl+\	
	Borders & lines	▸	

Step Three. Turn off Automatic Numbering and Automatic Bullet Lists

Some authors make a bullet list of their other books.

To create a bullet point, place your cursor at the beginning of the text, press down the Alt key and simultaneously press the number 7 on the keypad. Then insert a space before the first word of the text of that bullet point. Repeat the process for each bullet point on the list.

Step Four. Remove the Page Numbers and any Headers or Footers

Electronic documents don't use page numbers or header or footer text, since they are one long continuous stream of code.

For Word and Google Docs. Double click in the header or footer of your document where you have your page numbers. Delete the page number together with any text you may have in both the header and footer of your document.

Step Five. Remove the Forced Line Breaks and Paragraph Breaks

Many writers use the Enter key to add an extra line between paragraphs. All these extra breaks need to be removed.

Don't worry – we are going to add in extra spaces between paragraphs later. But for now, they must be taken out so that all your text is spaced the same way.

To find all forced line breaks and paragraph breaks, click the Paragraph mark in the Paragraph menu. This is also known as the Pilcrow mark.

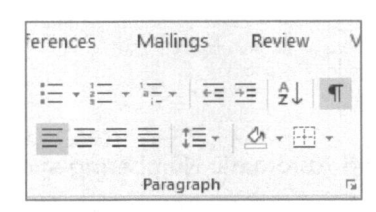

What you will now see are all the hidden paragraph breaks that you have inserted as you wrote your novel.

Now comes the difficult part.

You need to go through your document and delete any unwanted paragraph breaks or soft returns so that you only have one paragraph break at the end of each paragraph of text.

Step Six. Make sure all your chapters start on a new page

If you have been using paragraph breaks to force your new chapter to start on a new page, then the process you have gone through in step four will cause chaos when converted.

For Word and Google Docs. To make sure that each new chapter starts on a fresh page, use *the Ctrl +Enter* keys to insert a Page Break.

For Word. You can also use the *Layout* Tab in the menu, then *Breaks* then *Page* or the *Insert Page Break* function from the Pages menu in Word.

Step Seven. Remove Tabs

Many authors use tabs to indent the first word of each paragraph in the text. All these tabs must be deleted.

Step Eight. Remove Double Spaces

It is so easy to accidently press the space bar twice and insert a double space between letters or at the end of the sentence.

Unfortunately, double spaces really confuse the eBook conversion process and can destroy the smooth reading of your novel.

To make it easier, use the *Find and Replace* tool in Word to replace all the double spaces with a single space.

Go to the Editing menu, open the Replace box, and press the Space bar twice in the *Find What* field. Then go to the *Replace* With field and press the space only once.

You can *Replace All* or use the *Find Next* option to see where the error has occurred and replace the double space with a single space.

Step Nine. Images

Some authors like to use an image of:

• Their publishing or author brand on the title page of their book.

• An author photo in their About the Author Page.

- Book cover images of other books which are available now or on pre-order.

The correct way to add an image to the text in the front or back matter of your novel is to use the *Insert Image* function of your word processor.

To make sure that the image stays where you want it to go, it is best to place the image *In Line With Text* which locks it on a separate line between two paragraphs or text blocks.

Then centre the image on the page. This makes the image easier to see when the eBook is being read on a small screen, for example, a smart phone.

In Word. Click on the Image then the Image Layout Options.

The *In Line with Text* options should be shaded as live.

Here is an example where I have added an image of the book cover for the next book in a cozy mystery series at the back of the book.

In Google Docs. Click on the image and make sure that the *In line* option is live.

For example: This image was also centre aligned with the text.

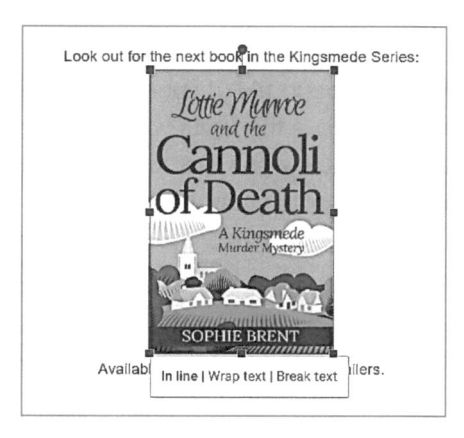

Important. If you have added a copy of your eBook cover to the first page of your document, you should remove this now.

The KDP system will link the eBook cover you upload into KDP with the text of your manuscript during the publishing phase. If you keep the cover image, then your reader will see two cover images which can be confusing. Best to keep to a standard text title page.

Righty. You should now have a "clean" version of your manuscript.

Time to add simple formatting instructions back in the document again so that it is ready to be uploaded onto KDP.

USING SIMPLE STYLES TO REBUILD THE STRUCTURE OF YOUR BOOK

Step One. Set the Normal Body Text Style

If you have removed all the unwanted formatting, the text of your novel will already be set to the "Normal" style. The best way to ensure that your text reads correctly as an eBook is to modify this Normal style to create one consistent style for font, paragraph indents and line spacing.

Font and Font Size

When you upload the .doc(x) file of your book into KDP, the Amazon system will update the fonts you have used to a default standard font and font size when it creates the reflowable eBook file. This allows the reader to change the font type and the font size on the reading device that they are using to read your book.

For example. Bookerly (serif) and Ember (sans serif), both Kindle-exclusive fonts, aim to provide the same style of modern print books while providing great readability on digital screens of all sizes.

To support this conversion process, I would recommend changing the Normal style of your novel to a serif font from the start which you know that KDP will accept. For most novels, readers will have a better reading experience of large amounts of text when you use a serif style font in font size 10 or 11.

Reminder. Serif fonts have small tails at the end of the letters. Non-serif fonts are cleaner and straighter in style. For example. Here are two serif fonts: Palatino and Georgia.

Using Bold and Italics. These can be used to add emphasis to text. Body text made up of entirely bold or italic text will be rejected.

Font Colour. Coloured text should also be changed back to standard black throughout the document.

How to change the Normal Style of your document.

Select a few paragraphs of text from a chapter in your novel. The style of that text will display in the Styles header bar.

In Word.

Change the font and font size of your text until you are happy with it.

In this example I want to change the font from Calibri 11point to Georgia 11point.

Click on the *Normal* style which should be highlighted then click on *Update Normal to Match Selection*.

Your Normal style for the entire document has now been changed.

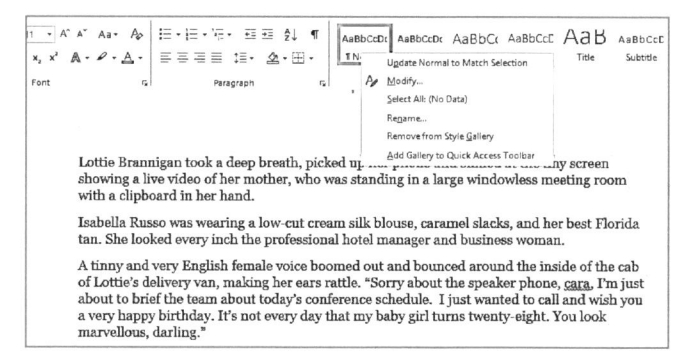

In Google Docs.

Select the text. Check that the header tells you that this is the Normal text style.

> Lottie Brannigan took a deep breath, picked up her phone and smiled at the tiny screen showing a live video of her mother, who was standing in a large windowless meeting room with a clipboard in her hand.
> Isabella Russo was wearing a low-cut cream silk blouse, caramel slacks, and her best Florida tan. She looked every inch the professional hotel manager and business woman.
> A tinny and very English female voice boomed out and bounced around the inside of the cab of Lottie's delivery van, making her ears rattle. "Sorry about the speaker phone, cara, I'm just about to brief the team about today's conference schedule. I just wanted to call and wish you a very happy birthday. It's not every day that my baby girl turns twenty-eight. You look marvellous, darling."

In this example the current font is Arial 11 point.

Let's change it to Georgia 11 point.

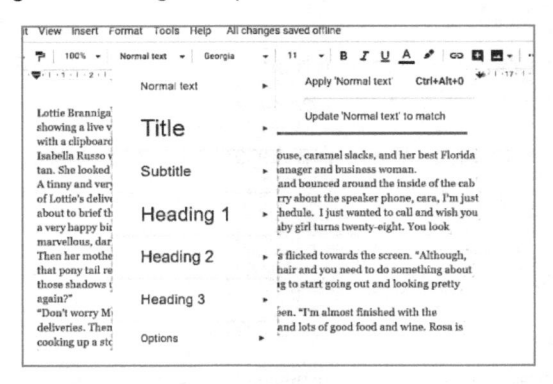

Click Update 'Normal text' to match.

Text Justification.

The text in reflowable Kindle eBooks is fully justified, both right and left, by default.

You can set the layout of the body text to be fully justified using the paragraph formatting tool and the Alignment options.

Replace manual paragraph tabs with auto indents for the first line of paragraphs

Most novelists prefer to indicate a new paragraph by indenting the text on the first line of each paragraph.

Instead of tabs you should use paragraph styles to set how much of an indent you want.

Using the same example of chapter text, I would suggest using a hanging indent for the first line of each paragraph of 0.3cm.

In Word.

Select a few paragraphs of body text from your novel.

Click on the **Paragraph** options in your header bar.

Then go to **General Alignment.** Use the dropdown arrow to change the Alignment from Left Aligned to Justified.

Then set the *Special First Line indentation* to 0.3cm (or the equivalent in the US) and click OK to insert the paragraph indent.

Some fiction authors prefer to use a larger first line indent of 0.4 cm so feel free to experiment with a large block of text to see how changing the first line indent impacts both the appearance and the reading experience of your novel.

See how your chapter looks and if you want a larger or smaller indent, simply repeat the process and change the width of the indent in the first line in the paragraph formatting styles.

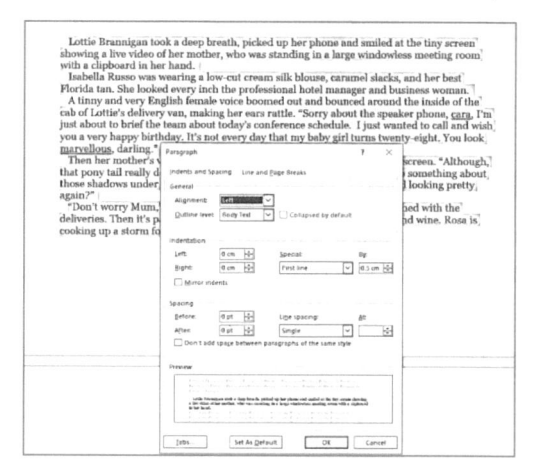

In Google Docs. Select a few paragraphs of text. Go to the *Format* option in the header bar, then *Align and Indent*.

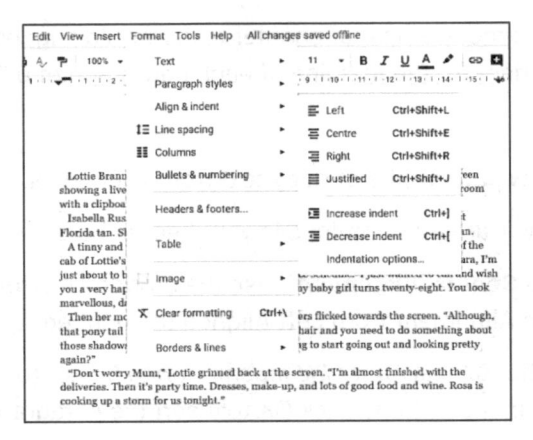

Click on the Justified option on the right sidebar.

Then select the *Indentation Options* and then *Special, First Line* and set the indent you prefer.

Step Two. Set the Chapter Heading Style

It is essential that you tell the Kindle KDP where your chapters or page titles are so that the system can create an automatic table of contents for you.

Heading 1 Style.

All chapter titles and section/page headings should be marked as Header 1 style if you want them to be included in the Table of Contents of your eBook.

The easiest thing to do is to work through your text and change any heading that you wish to have in your table of contents to the Heading 1 style.

This includes the header title text of:

Front Matter. About the Book, Note from the Author if you have one – but not the Table of Contents.

Body Text. Every Chapter Title.

Back Matter. Any Acknowledgements. Other Books by the Author. About the Author page. The Copyright page.

The process for assigning all header styles is the same.

In both Word and Google Docs, simply click at the chapter or page heading and select Heading 1 style.

For example.

In Word. The chapter one heading is currently in Normal and left aligned.

In Google docs.

Select the chapter heading. Click on the *Normal text* header and click the down arrow to *select Heading 1*, then Apply *'Heading 1'*.

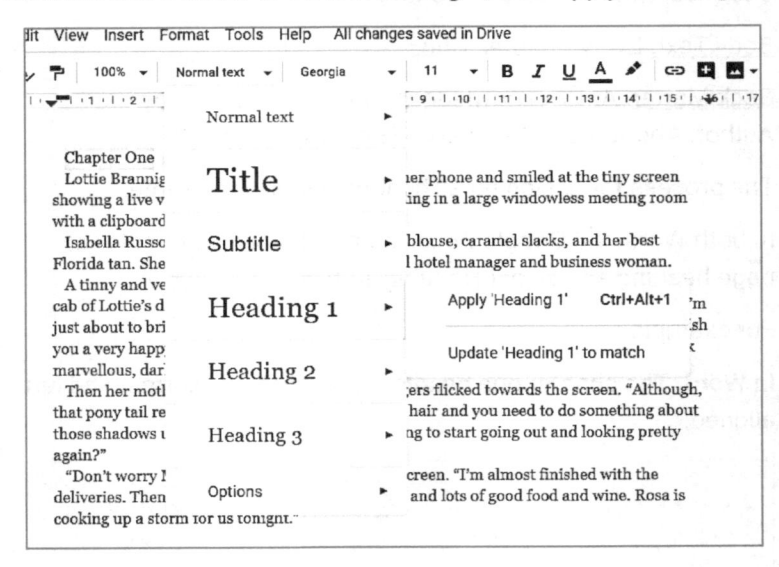

You can now update the font and font size of the chapter headings and change the alignment. For example, if you want to place your chapter heading in the centre of the page.

Many authors also prefer to have a line space after the chapter heading.

To do this, you can make the change in your document, select the heading text and apply the "Update Heading 1 to match" in the style menu. Or go into the style menu and change the settings for Heading 1 using the Format Font and Paragraph menus.

Now work through the document and apply the saved Heading 1 style to every chapter title and page title that you want to be included in the table of contents for your book.

Step Three. Create an Automatic Clickable/Hyperlinked Table of Contents

Once you have created Heading styles for your document, you can use the word processing software to scan your document and create a list of the headings as a Table of Contents for your document. The top level of the list will be Heading 1 followed by Heading 2 and 3 etc. but you can select how many levels you want in the Table of Contents and which Headings are to be included. For short fiction, it will be level one, Heading 1.

To Create the Automatic Table of Contents

The simplest and fastest way to create a Table of Contents for your eBook is to use the word processing software to generate one for you. You can be confident that the page location will always be correct and if you make changes to the text, it only takes one click to update the contents.

Put your cursor in the front matter of the document where you want to insert the table of contents, usually just before the main text. Type in the word Contents or Table of Contents and give it a Normal style – you don't usually want the Table of Contents to be in the listing.

In Word.

• Go to the References tab in the header bar.

• Click on Table of Contents.

• Then select the Custom Table of Contents option at the bottom of the box.

Uncheck "Show page numbers".

Check "Use hyperlinks instead of page numbers".

• Go to General. Show levels

For fiction writers, this will usually be 1 level (Heading 1) unless your novel is divided into parts, in which case change this to 2.

• Click on "Options"

Scroll down all the styles that you can use to build a Table of Contents (TOC). **Select Heading 1** as TOC level 1.

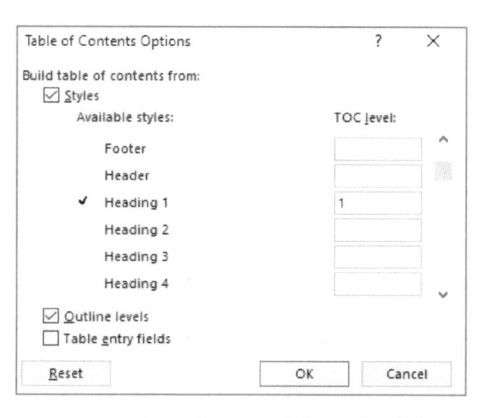

[Table of Contents Options dialog box showing: Build table of contents from Styles, Available styles (Footer, Header, Heading 1 ✓ with TOC level 1, Heading 2, Heading 3, Heading 4), Outline levels checked, Table entry fields unchecked, with Reset, OK, and Cancel buttons.]

• If you only want to use Heading 1, delete the (1) number against any other style that may be listed as an option.

• Click OK. The software will now detect all of the headings that you have selected and list that text with a hyperlink associated with the position of that header text in your document.

Modifying the Table of Contents Style

In Word.

• Go to the References tab in the header bar.

• Click on Table of Contents. Then use the down arrow to select Custom Table of Contents option at the bottom of the box.

• To change the font and font size used, select the Modify Option. This will take you to the font option menu and you can select any font combination that you wish.

To update the table of contents at any time, simply click on the table and right click if you are using a mouse. Then click on Update Field.

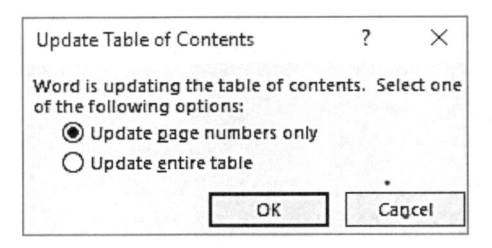

Inserting a Table of Contents in Google Docs.

• Place your cursor in the position where you want the Table of Contents.

• Go to Insert in the Editing mode, then Table of Contents.

• Select the option which will show blue bars – these will be hyperlinked locations. [Page numbers are for print books.]

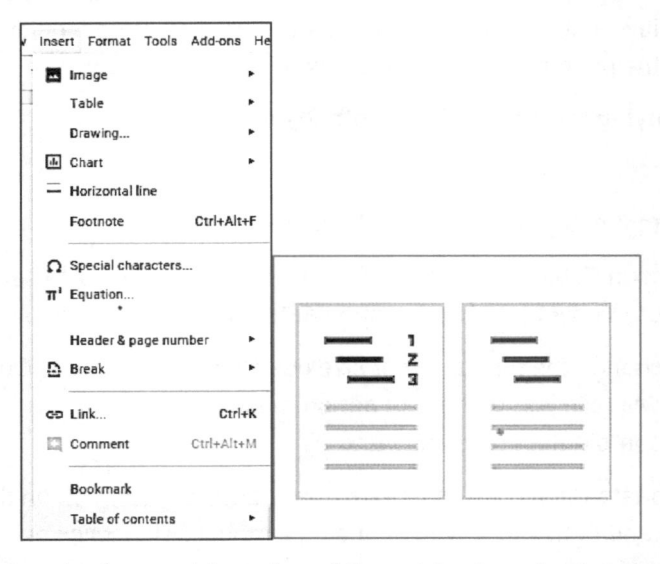

• Change the font and font size of the entries by selecting the entire table of contents then clicking on the font options in the header.

If you make changes to your document that affect the table of contents, you can update the table of contents by right clicking the table of contents and choosing **Update Field**.

This will update the hyperlinked location of the header in an electronic document.

SAVE your document as a new .docx file.

Great! Now save your formatted document as a **.docx format file** which is ready to be converted into a Kindle eBook. This is the preferred document type.

For more information go here>
https://kdp.amazon.com/en_US/help/topic/G200634390

Step Four. Preview and Validate your document before uploading

The Amazon Kindle Previewer Tool

Amazon have provided an excellent free preview tool for independently published authors and I would recommend that you check your document using the Kindle Previewer before you start the publishing process inside KDP.

Kindle Previewer helps you preview and validate how your books will appear when delivered to Kindle customers before you publish.

The latest version of Kindle Previewer has the full Enhanced Typesetting features so that you can check the appearance of images, tables, font alignments, word spacing, hyphenation and text features.

Kindle Previewer is available for Windows and Mac OS X.

Download the most recent version of Kindle Previewer through the link at

https://www.amazon.com/gp/feature.html/?docId=1000765261

Take the time to scan the features of this powerful previewer tool.

One of the key benefits of Kindle Previewer is that you can see what your document will look like on any kind of reading device before you upload it onto KDP. Simply use the toggle switch under Device Type to change the device and the orientation of the device.

You can change the font, font size and navigate within your document.

This is particularly useful if you are a non-fiction writer and have included images, charts and tables in your document. Many readers prefer to read books on smart phones and tablets. This is your opportunity to see how your document will appear to readers on small, narrow screens.

To load a text document onto the Kindle Previewer:

Go to File in the top left menu bar.

Click on Open Book. This will take you to your document folders where you can find your manuscript.

It can take a few minutes for the document to be converted into a Kindle eBook and display on the previewer screen.

<u>Key Elements to check using Kindle Previewer</u>

1. The Cover pages. Does the text appear in the centre of the page? Is there a clear separation between the title and the author name? It is always useful to test this in the smart phone device option.

The text will display differently on a Kindle E-reader as opposed to the Kindle app.

2. The Hyperlinked Table of Contents is a key part of any electronic book.

Does every one of the chapter headings link through to the correct location in the document?

As an additional check toggle the Table of Contents option to open up the display.

Carefully check that every chapter heading and page heading that you want to be included in the Table of Contents is listed. If one is missing, go back to your text document, change the heading style to Heading 1 as appropriate, then save the document as a new file and upload it again into the Previewer.

3. Navigation inside the document

The aim is to simulate the same reading experience as someone buying your book.

Go to the Navigation tab in the top menu bar.

Check that each of the links takes the reader to the correct location in the book.

#4. The Appearance of the text

Do all the chapter headings look the same? They should do if you have used the Header 1 style. One thing to check is the spacing between the heading and the first line of text.

Body text alignment. The text should automatically be fully justified with the small indent that you created at the start of each new paragraph.

Blank pages. It is very easy to accidently insert a page break and create a blank page which will confuse readers.

Scene Break Symbols. If you have used symbols to introduce a scene break [usually three asterisks] with a space above and below the symbols, check that the spacing is not too large and that the symbols are centred. These will look different according to the font the reader has selected on their device.

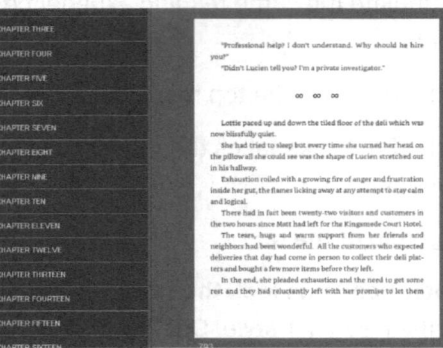

Hyperlinks in the text and Images

If you have added links in the text to, for example, your website URL or your Amazon page so that readers can review the work, check that all the hyperlinks are working.

Images should appear central and large enough to be seen but not overwhelm the page relative to the text size.

One final check. Read through your book on the screen.

It is amazing how many tiny things slip through the editing and proofreading process, no matter how many times you have read the contents.

This is your final check to make sure that the content is the best that you can make it.

In the past, I have moved chapters around and changed chapter breaks in fiction books so that the text reads more smoothly.

It only takes a few minutes to update the text and reload it onto the Kindle Previewer.

This is your book! You should be proud of your work and excited to share it with readers worldwide.

Happy? Then save a new master file of your document and get ready to publish.

PART FIVE. PUBLISHING ON AMAZON

19. Publish Your eBook on KDP

SO WHERE DO YOU START?

Log onto your Amazon KDP account to publish your Kindle eBook.

Your Kindle Direct Publishing Account

If you don't already have a KDP account, follow the instructions on the home page to set-up your account, tax information and payment details. For example. https://kdp.amazon.com/en_US

You will be taken to a Bookshelf page where you can **Create a New Title**.

Click on + Kindle eBook

```
Create a New Title
  +           ● Book Content: You can upload a manuscript, or use our free creation tools to create children's books, educational content, comics, and
Kindle eBook    manga. Get started with Kindle content creation tools.
              ● Book Cover: You can use our online Cover Creator, or upload a cover of your own. Creating a great cover.
              ● Description, Keywords and Categories: Tell readers about your book and help them find it on Amazon.
  +           ● ISBN: Get a free ISBN to publish your paperback. Kindle eBooks don't need one. More about ISBNs.
Paperback     See all Getting Started tips ›
```

Kindle eBook Details Page

Start working down the page, completing each section in turn until you have a complete profile for your book.

• Language.

• Book Title and any Subtitle.

• Series. The Series link is particularly useful is you are considering making your novel part of a new or existing series of linked novels.

You can return to this page at any time and update the series information for the Kindle store book page for this novel.

20. Book Descriptions, Keywords and Categories

OPTIMISING THE BOOK DETAILS FOR ONLINE PUBLISHING

The first thing to recognise is that Amazon is a search engine.

The two key elements to this functionality are the computer algorithm Amazon uses to rank your book and the metadata for your book.

All of your marketing efforts have to be focused on helping Amazon to recognise that your book is selling well, so that the book pops up on the *Also Read* and *Hot Releases* lists and is not lost in the desert with the thousands of other romance titles already out there.

Amazon will also look for keywords in your book title and book description, and link those into the algorithm so that your marketing and publishing strategy will place your romance on one of the many bestseller charts.

The Amazon systems will then take over and do the marketing for you.

That's why you only have limited control over where your romance will sit on the Kindle Store. Amazon will slot it into a virtual shelf based on all of the information about that book file.

Don't be surprised if you see your book come up on a print romance chart when all you have available is an electronic eBook.

Amazon only makes money when you make a sale, so it is in their best interest to help readers find your book. Work with the system and it will work for you.

In a brick and mortar traditional bookstore you can browse the shelves which are usually organised by genre and then by the author name.

Online book distributors work in the same way – except that they are essentially huge computer databases. Book are data files which are sorted according to the information you give them about your book.

The keywords are the words that readers use to search for books on the Kindle store – they want to find romances on a certain shelf. So, it is worth spending time creating keywords which will help Amazon to pull up your romance for that combination of keywords.

For people to find your book you need to have a keyword rich title and book description, your so-called meta data.

THE BOOK DESCRIPTION AND ANY SUBTITLE ON EBOOK OR THE BACK-COVER BLURB.

You have spent weeks or months writing this book and now comes the fun part – telling your ideal audience all about it!

Before you write the book details for your book and load them onto Kindle Direct Publishing take the time to put yourself into the position of a casual browser to the online bookstore.

I want to be enticed into reading this book by the anticipation of an exciting and or romantic emotional journey.

The only place I will find that is from the Book Description and the Additional material the author has added about the book.

Does your book description have a compelling and irresistible hook with keywords which link to your cover image? Is the subtitle short, memorable and irresistible?

Is the book description easy to understand? Remember – this will be scanned by browsers to the online bookstore who are intrigued by the cover art.

Think about reading the description on the flap of a dust jacket or on the back cover of a printed book. How would you capture the essence of your book in a few sentences?

This will be the core information that is available for browsers scanning the digital shelves at the online bookstores.

Some online platforms ask for a short description which will be displayed next to the image, and a longer paragraph for the book page.

Use the Book description and any subtitles to make the compelling short pitch. If you are on Kindle eBooks, you can then use the Author Central feature to add lots more information and editorial reviews. Make me a promise. Show me that this book will be worth my time.

Then see if you can incorporate genre and niche keywords organically into that book description.

Question. How can I make sure that readers would love my book know that it even exists?

Answer. Strategy: Help readers to find my book

Incorporate Keywords in your Book Details for Search Engine Optimisation

The online publishing platforms will search the information you provide for your book and try and match it with the search criteria that readers are typing in.

RECOMMENDED CATEGORY LINKED KEYWORDS

KEYWORDS MATTER

Keywords — Enter up to 7 search keywords that describe your book. How do I choose keywords?

Your Keywords (Optional)

Categories — Choose up to two browse categories. Why are categories important?

Set Categories

When you publish on Kindle Direct Publishing [KDP] you can type in a maximum of seven keywords and phrases.

Don't rush to type in the first words that you think matches your book. Keywords are magical search terms and you should research them in detail.

When a reader goes onto the Kindle Store and types in a few words into the Search box, a whole list of options will appear in a drop-down list for that reader to help them fine tune their search.

For example, if you go to a blank Kindle Store eBook bestseller search and type the word '*Amish Romance*,' then Amazon will automatically give you a drop-down list of the top ten words and phrases that are the most popular search words that readers have used to find eBooks about this subgenre. These include:

- Amish romance kindle books
- Amish romance fiction
- Amish romance novels

- Free Amish romance novels
- Christian Amish romance
- Free Amish romance
- Amish romance secrets
- Amish romance books
- Amish romance series.

They are the ten keywords that readers use most often, so why not use those exact keyword strings in your seven keywords and phrases?

Make it easy for Amazon to point readers to your books. Let the search engine functionality do the hard work for you.

You may have seen that for some romance categories there are sometimes additional search features called 'Themes' on the left-hand side of the page. These are also based on the keywords.

When you are on the first page of KDP, where you enter your book information, there is a link to a page called 'Selecting Book Categories.'

Scroll down to Romance and you will see a long list of possibilities.

So, for an Amish Romance you might choose: Romance/Inspirational/Amish and Romance/Inspirational/General or perhaps the Romance/Holidays option if you have a seasonal book.

These are specific to Amazon.com in the US, but you can see the range available.

Always try and incorporate as many of those search phrases as you can into your seven keywords. If you can get them into the title or subtitle of your book, even better!

So instead of using single words, use keywords strings when you publish.

Make a list of the ideal strings and likely search phrases by researching all of the phrases which match your book, match them to the popular search suggestions that Amazon comes up with and then use some of these in your book description and some in the keyword listing.

If you publish on Amazon KDP you should be aware that there are certain categories where there are "keyword requirements."

The full list is here>>>

https://kdp.amazon.com/en_US/help/topic/G200652170

If Amazon KDP recommends keywords in specific categories, then this is the first place I should go to.

NOTE - there are two lists. One for Amazon.com and one for Amazon.co.uk. This is because categories may have different names on these two Kindle Stores and there can be different subcategories.

ORGANIC SEARCH

If you open up the home page on your local Kindle Store on Amazon.com and type the word "romance" into the search bar, Amazon will instantly give you a pre-populated drop-down list with all of the search terms that other readers have already typed in.

When you click on any of these options, Amazon will now search the database and match up all the keywords you have given it when you published the book to find books for this reader.

How can we make our books stand out so that readers can find them?

Our goal is to find some way of bringing our books to the attention of readers and rank our work higher in the search engine than other books.

The more keywords you have that match – the more likely it is that your book will pop up in the results page.

THERE ARE FOUR PLACES WHERE YOU CAN PLACE KEYWORDS TO MAKE YOUR BOOK EASY TO FIND FOR YOUR IDEAL READER.

#1. **The Title** of the book.

#2. **The Subtitle**. This is why so many eBooks have keyword rich subtitles which seem unnecessary but are essential to help readers find your book – but don't go over the top and have huge long lists of words.

#3. **The Book Description.** Your aim should be to incorporate as many keywords as possible into the book description but make it feel natural and easy to read.

#4. **The Keywords and keyword strings** in the keywords section of KDP which you use to set-up your book. You can use up to 7 search keywords to describe your book.

Tom Morkes has an excellent article on how you can optimise keywords and a 60-minute video on this topic which you can find here>> https://tommorkes.com/kindle-seo/

"*Amazon Kindle SEO is all about ranking your book higher than other books for your keywords.*" Tom Morkes

FORMATTING THE BOOK DESCRIPTION.

How to use HTML code to make your description look better

HTML tags are the hidden keywords within a web page that define how the browser must format and display the content.

The tags usually start with a <symbol> at the beginning of the text and </symbol> at the end. For example. <h1> indicates that the text should be displayed as a large Header One. </h1> closes out the formatting and tells the browser to return to Normal font.

You should also try to keep the text on your Amazon (or other sales page) neat and tidy by using bold text, italics and headings. One way to make your book details stand out is to add in some code around the text.

The best idea is to keep it super simple.

To make your text bold, insert <b> in front of the text, and then close it with </b>.

To make your text stand out in Amazon orange, insert <h2> at the beginning of your header, and close it with </h2>. These are additive, so if you wanted a bold orange header, use both pieces of code.

<h2><b>Are you ready to learn how to transform your Romance eBook sales?</b></h2>

You can always change this at any time by going back into KDP if you don't like how the description appears on the Kindle Store.

You can then check what that book description looks like in text, using sites such as: https://ablurb.github.io/.

SUPPORTED HTML FOR BOOK DESCRIPTION

Amazon Kindle Direct Publishing allows you to use the following html tags inside your book description area (up to date as of March 2020)

This page includes a complete list of HTML tags supported in the book description field. To avoid formatting errors, please close your HTML tags. For example, to close this tag for bold text <b>, you need to add </b>, which prevents the rest of your content from appearing as bold text.

Open HTML tag	Close HTML tag	Description
<b>	</b>	Formats enclosed text as bold
 	</br>	Creates a line break
<em>	</em>	Emphasizes the enclosed text. Generally formatted as italic.
<h4> to <h6>	</h4> to </h6>	Formats enclosed text as a section heading: <h4> (largest) through <h6> (smallest). <h1>, <h2>, and <h3> aren't supported.
<i>	</i>	Formats enclosed text as italic
<li>	</li>	Identifies an item in an ordered (numbered) or unordered (bulleted) list
<ol>	</ol>	Creates a numbered list from enclosed items, each of which is identified by a <li> tag
<ul>	</ul>	Creates a bulleted list from enclosed items, each of which is identified by a <li> tag
<p>	</p>	Defines a paragraph of text with the first line indented. Creates a line break at the end of the enclosed text.
<pre>	</pre>	Defines pre-formatted text
<u>	</u>	Formats enclosed text as underlined
<strong>	</strong>	Formats enclosed text as bold. See also <b>.
<q>	</q>	Encloses text in quotes.

When your eBook page is live on the Kindle store, it is always a good idea to check the book description. You can edit the description at any time by coming back to this Book Details page.

CATEGORIES AND SUB-CATEGORIES

We covered this topic in-depth earlier in this book, but now you have finished your manuscript you want to reconsider which two main categories and/or subcategories are the best fit for your work. Remember! Be strategic. Your goal must be to help readers to find your work through the Amazon search engine.

THE NEXT ENTRY ON THE BOOKS DETAILS PAGE IS CATEGORIES.

One of the benefits of digital publishing is that Amazon and other online publishing platforms have created virtual bookstore shelves with main categories, sub-categories and sub-sub-categories where readers can browse and find the precise book that they are looking for.

Digital publishing makes "niche" publishing viable again.

Assigning Categories for eBooks and Print Books

The first thing to recognise is that "Amazon is less of a store and more of a search engine." (Penny Sansevieri, 2015)

Make your book more discoverable for readers by placing it in the categories that match it best.

YOU ARE ALLOWED TO USE TWO CATEGORIES FOR EACH BOOK.

I think of categories as virtual bookshelves on the Amazon store.

Now you need to tell Amazon which shelf your book belongs on.

The easiest thing to do is to research books on the Amazon Kindle store which are the closest match to your book and use the same two categories if you can.

Note. Your local Kindle store may not use the same categories as the USA category selection, so research your local Amazon store to ensure that you have the best category fit.

```
Choose up to two categories:                                    ×

Choose categories (up to two):

    ⊞ Fiction
    ⊞ Nonfiction
    ⊞ Juvenile Fiction
    ⊞ Juvenile Nonfiction
    ⊞ Comics & Graphic Novels
    ⊞ Education & Reference
    ⊞ Literary Collections
    ☐ Non-Classifiable


Selected categories:



                                              Cancel    Save
```

Each of these Major Categories expands down into many subcategories which may further expand into sub-subcategories and more niche categories.

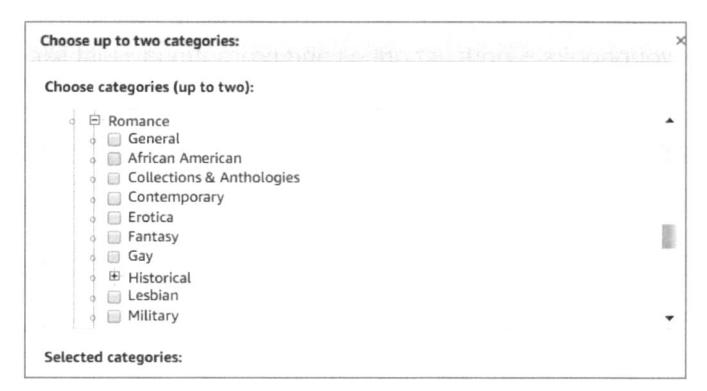

```
Choose up to two categories:                                    ×

Choose categories (up to two):

    ⊟ Romance                                                ▲
        ☐ General
        ☐ African American
        ☐ Collections & Anthologies
        ☐ Contemporary
        ☐ Erotica
        ☐ Fantasy
        ☐ Gay
      ⊞ Historical
        ☐ Lesbian
        ☐ Military                                           ▼

Selected categories:
```

Use the scrollbar to find the two romance categories that are the best fit for your work.

21. Pricing

BE STRATEGIC WHEN IT COME TO THE PRICE OF YOUR BOOK

Many independent authors tend to focus on the number of copies they sell and the corresponding sales rank of their books.

This is totally fine, but don't forget that author income is a function of three major variables: The number of copies sold × book price × royalty rate.

The royalty rate with Amazon KDP is set to a maximum of 70% for titles between $2.99 and 9.99 and 35% outside this range.

As a self-publishing author, you are fully in charge of the list prices for your books – both list prices and promotions –just like a major publishing company would do.

THREE KEY QUESTIONS BEFORE YOU SET YOUR BOOK'S PRICE

There are three key questions you must ask yourself before you set the list price for your book:

1. WHO IS YOUR AUDIENCE?

Romance readers demand very competitive prices for their romance fiction and you have to recognise that. Romance Kindle eBooks have the lowest average price in the US Kindle store, although this varies from niche to niche.

2. WHAT IS THE VALUE OF MY BOOK AND HOW IS IT POSITIONED?

This question refers to the book itself and to the whole positioning of your author brand (if you have one.) Is your book a debut 20,000-word novella or a boxed set with a ten-part series?

Do you have a tribe of devoted followers who cannot wait to read the next volume in your bestselling series? Or is this a debut book and you don't have a large author brand or platform?

3. WHAT IS THE PRICE RANGE OF SIMILAR BOOKS IN YOUR CATEGORY?

Research the top titles in the bestseller chart for your category to get a feel for how your eBook should be priced.

Take a look at the other eBooks of the same length which will be on the shelf next to yours in the same category and subcategory, so that you know exactly what you are competing against on price.

The easiest way to do this is simply write down the number of pages and the price for the top 20 titles in your chosen two niches.

For short fiction the price is usually 99 cents to $2.99 but it is always a good idea to check.

KINDLE SELECT

One of the options you can select when you upload a book onto the Amazon Kindle Direct Publishing platform [KDP] is to enrol the book in Kindle Select, in addition to normal distribution to Amazon online stores.

Kindle Select offers a number of benefits to independently published authors.

1. DISTRIBUTION

Your book will be shared with readers through the Kindle Unlimited and the Kindle Owners' Lending Library, as well as on Amazon Kindle stores.

Kindle Unlimited is a subscription service for readers where they pay one monthly fee and they can download as many eBooks as they want.

The Kindle Owners' Lending Library is a collection of books that Amazon curates. Amazon Prime members who own a Kindle can choose one book from the library each month with no due dates.

Effectively you are expanding your audience and readership by enrolling your book in Kindle Select. These readers will not buy your book. Genre fiction fans, such as mystery and romance readers, are prolific consumers of eBooks, and programs like Kindle Unlimited give them access to as many books as they want.

2. EXTRA PAYMENTS

The reader does not buy your book, so you are not paid the purchase or download price. Instead, every time a reader actively reads a page in one of your books, you get paid a share of a KDP Select Global Fund. You are paid by the total number of pages read in any given month. Currently this is about 0.5 cents US a page, but this can change monthly.

Each author receives a portion of the Global Fund proportional to how many pages of their titles were read. The more pages read the bigger the pay-out.

Hence the popularity of Boxed Sets of books. More pages. More Kindle Select payments.

3. SPECIAL KINDLE SELECT PROMOTIONAL OPPORTUNITIES

There are two extra promotional tools which are only available for eBooks enrolled in Kindle Select:

*Kindle Countdown Deals, time-bound promotional discounting for your book while earning royalties at list price, and

*Free Book Promotion where you can offer your book for free for up to 5 days out of each 90-day KDP Select enrolment period. Because your book is available for free during a free book promotion, you won't receive royalties for it while the promotion runs. You can run all 5 days at once, go one day at a time, or offer your book free for multiple days in a row. This can be particularly useful at a 'soft launch' of your book where you want readers to download a free review copy.

For more information about Kindle Unlimited and the Kindle Owners' Lending Library, go to the Kindle Direct Publishing website.

THE MAIN DISADVANTAGE OF ENROLLING IN KINDLE SELECT

You must agree to publish that eBook exclusively with Amazon for a period of 90 days. You cannot therefore make the eBook available on other digital publishing platforms like Kobo, Apple, Barnes and Noble, Google Play etc. But you can distribute printed copies.

There are romance readers who do not want to read a Kindle book and prefer to read on their Kobo eReader or buy their book on Apple iBooks or other alternatives.

Some authors feel uncomfortable putting all their eggs in one basket and ignoring the opportunities to expand their audience outside of Amazon.

CONCLUSIONS?

For me it comes down to one word: **Discoverability.**

Where are my readers most likely to go to find new books to read? For me, the answer is Amazon, which is now one of the largest product search engines in the world.

I want and need to get my book in front of readers and help them to know that it exists. They won't have heard of me or my past work. It is all down to organic searches and using search engines such as Amazon to make my book cover and title pop up.

So, I plan to launch this book on Amazon and enrol in Kindle Select.

22. Pre-Orders

Why Bother with Creating a Pre-Order for a Kindle eBook?

PUBLICATION SCHEDULE

Realistically I always allow 5 working days for the new book details to load onto KDP and for the book page to appear on Amazon. By setting a specific release date, this gives me time to check that the book details look the way I want, and I can amend the book description and meta data on the book page if needed. You will need a good book cover and description, hot categories and keywords etc. ready asap.

HOT NEW RELEASES CHART

If anyone buys a copy of the book when it is in pre-order on Amazon, the sale is recorded on that day, which means that it kicks off the Amazon algorithm. The boost pre-launch can kick the book into the Hot New Releases Chart for that niche subcategory. [This contrasts with many other online publishing platforms where the pre-order sales are accumulated and counted on the launch day.]

AMAZON AUTHOR CENTRAL

It is essential to have an author account on Amazon author central, especially if you are new to Amazon or want to create a new account on Amazon Author Central for anew pen name. To do this, you need to have a book to claim, even if it is on pre-order. Note – you will have to create accounts in the key Amazon

Kindle stores where your books will be sold. The information is not automatically shared across the local stores.

ADVANCE REVIEW QUOTES AND TESTIMONIALS

When the book goes live it is great to have some endorsements and advance reviews you can add to the book description as Editorial Reviews inside Amazon Author Central.

These Editorial reviews will be listed on the book page, separately from reader reviews, and help to reassure readers that they will not be wasting their time and money investing in your book.

LINK URL FOR THE BOOK

You can link to the specific pre-order page in the pre-launch marketing campaign and social media posts.

GOODREADS

Many authors create an author profile on Goodreads. To do that you need to link to a book that you have published.

THERE ARE THREE THINGS TO WATCH OUT FOR WITH PRE-ORDERS

#1. Submission Timelines

At this point in the publishing process it is possible to upload a draft version of your manuscript, then complete the final changes to your text and load the final finished version of the text during the time window before the book is released as a pre-order.

Many authors do not notice that there is an official **submission deadline**, when the document you have loaded will be locked and moved into the Amazon quality review process before going on sale.

The system will give you regular updates telling you how long you have before the submission deadline, but this is a fixed cut-off point and you will be blocked from uploading any new version of your text on or after this date.

I would recommend that you must be ready to upload a final master copy of your formatted manuscript at least a week before the pre-order release date.

If you miss the submission date, your customers/readers will be sent the draft version of your book they ordered when they placed the pre-order, complete with all of the mistakes and notes and errors that you had planned to change in the final version.

Yes, you can upload a new copy of the book as soon as the book goes live, but what would you think if you have purchased a book which is full of errors and typos?

If your miss your pre-order window and a rough draft goes live, readers might leave negative reviews that will impact sales later. So always load a publication ready draft if you can.

#2. Sales Ranking

My process is that I don't promote or share the link to the pre-order book until I start the pre-launch campaign. The goal is to focus sales in a short time period just before and just after launch – maximising the sales ranking. That's why I recommend scheduling the pre-order date no more than two weeks before the target launch date. If you are looking for that magical 'bestseller' sticker, you won't get it if all of your pals ordered the book during pre-order.

#3. Reviews

Keep in mind that ARC readers can't review a pre-order book on Amazon.

23. KDP Print Paperbacks

Generally speaking, most of your readers will prefer to read short romance fiction in electronic format on their Kindle or Kindle app. Once your romance has some traction and is selling well, extend the shelf life by creating a print version.

But there is a market for print format books for:

• Short Novels

• Collections of Novellas

• Series of linked Short Stories, Novellas or Short Novels in Boxed Sets.

I have been amazed at how many authors prefer a print version of my books as opposed to an eBook. Use the KDP paperback option to publish the print version if you have not already done so.

WILL PRINT BOOKS BE WORTH IT?

For most independent authors, who do not have an extensive following and several thousand eBooks sales under their belts, the time and money you invest in creating a printed version of your book will not be repaid through book sales.

Your print-on-demand book will not be stocked in bookstores

As writers I am sure that we all adore spending time in bookstores and would love to see our work stocked on those shelves, waiting for browsers to pick them up.

The sad truth is that bookstores are simply not geared up to take self-published books. Unless your book is already a bestseller, then they find it easier to spend time with the sales reps who want them to stock the latest blockbuster releases and distribution channels which deliver books like clockwork.

This is especially true for the large chains where the book buying decisions are made centrally and local managers have little flexibility.

For most authors the online bookstores are going to be the first place that readers go to find your book and that is where you should focus your efforts.

You should therefore be very clear about why it is important to have your book in print, and temper that goal with very realistic and practical expectations about potential sales.

SO WHY BOTHER WITH A PRINT FORMAT OF YOUR NOVEL?

Some **readers** will always prefer to read a printed book, and this could be the best publishing model for your novel. You know your readers and you know that this is the way they want to read books.

If you write historical fiction for example, many of your readers will not use computers or eBook readers.

Book groups prefer printed books

Marketing. It makes it easy to give away promotional samples and competition prizes at sites like Goodreads.com. Some book reviewers also prefer a printed book.

Price Comparison. If you have a high price printed option for your book listed at the same time as your eBook, this will make your eBook seem very good value in comparison.

You can sell paperbacks at author events and writing conferences. Fellow writers love printed books.

Personal satisfaction. This is one case where the heart can outweigh the decisions of the head. There is nothing like holding a copy of a printed book that you have written which has your name or pen name on the cover, and then seeing your book stacked on your bookshelves. It really is a delightful feeling of accomplishment and self-gratification.

Your family and friends may be delighted that you have self-published your work in electronic form but having a real book to hold is very different and validating.

DISADVANTAGES

Sales. If you are writing commercial genre fiction, then most of your readers will prefer the instant gratification of an eBook that they can download in seconds. Don't expect massive paperback sales of a mainstream romance or crime novel.

Discount to book sellers. All sellers of printed book expect something like 40% trade discount and this has to come off the sales income before the author profit can be calculated. Which is why most self-published printed books are expensive compared to mass produced print books. This is one of the reasons most romance author opt for a print on demand service like KDP Print Paperbacks.

Cover Design Costs. You will need to create a spine and back cover image for your printed book, which are additional costs.

If you already have an eBook cover most of the DIY publishers have software which allows you to create a spine and back cover image online, or you can go back to the person who designed your eBook cover.

You will need to purchase an ISBN for each print format of your book, since this is used as the tracking system for your book in all stages of the distribution and publication process.

This is optional if you only want to sell your books through Print on Demand on Amazon Paperbacks. The downside is that with Amazon Paperbacks, the book will be listed as "Independently Published."

Interior Book Design costs. The layout of printed book is completely different from the continuous flow of eBooks and this will take additional formatting time, depending on the publishing platform you select. Many authors hire professionals to design the interior of the book, or buy pre-formatted templates, and you can find out more about this on sites like TheBookDesigner.com. You can find a freelancer to do this for you on Fiver.com.

Quality. The quality of paper and the choice of publishing options and book dimensions can be bewildering, and they will impact the finish quality of your printed book.

Difficult to change the printed book. No matter how many times you have proofread your manuscript, you will find small errors and typos, and readers will let you know! Digital print on demand can get around this, by allowing you to update your master digital file, but small presses will print what you give them. Some authors wait a few months before creating a printed format for this reason.

You cannot do this on your own. A physical book will need to be printed using the paper quality and paper size [known as trim size] that you select, and then bound as a paperback or hardback with the type of cover you select. This really is couture book production. Which has the plus of being unique, but all of that technology and physical handling costs money, so inevitably you either have to pay to have these books printed or take a smaller percentage royalty relative to an eBook. This pushes up the list price you have to ask for the print book.

EBook first, then consider print. There are some authors who wait until they have tested the market for their eBook before investing in the additional costs of producing a print book and pay for those costs from the income from their eBooks. They are essentially waiting to see if there are enough sales to justify the costs.

Steep Learning Curve. Print format books do take time to format, design, layout and optimise for print. That time could well be spent writing the next book and then the next.

KDP PRINT PAPERBACKS

To keep the process as simple as possible, I recommend KDP Print Paperbacks. It is an ideal, no-risk, option for authors who have not self-published before, and who are therefore unsure of the potential sales of their book, or who want to offer their readers the choice of an electronic or print book, or both.

There are no set-up fees and a very comprehensive set of design and production and publication tools for the independent publisher.

Benefits of using KDP Print.

• You can consolidate the eBook and Print book formats for your book at the same time. If you enroll for the Amazon Kindle Matchbook program, you can offer anyone who buys a copy of the printed book, the electronic copy of the same book for free or at a very low cost. This is an excellent marketing opportunity which is unique to Amazon.

• You can review a digital proof of your Print on Demand book before it is fully approved for shipment, and you will receive a proof copy.

• Global reach and extensive print technology. Fast turnaround on orders and shipping using the Amazon delivery service.

• Great option for authors who may not sell many copies but needs to be in print, since there are no upfront costs.

• Very user friendly and very comprehensive website offering lots of detailed instructions on how to create your printed books, and resource articles.

• You set the pricing structure and control the metadata about your book.

• The Print on Demand service covers a wide range of book trim sizes, papers, layout, cover options and colour printing. Most authors chose the 5.25 inches by 8 inches or 6 x 9 inches with cream paper and a matt cover. But there is also an option to create a custom book size.

• You are given the choice of buying an ISBN, or not. If you do not purchase an ISBN of your own, then KDP Print will provide one free of charge, but then they will be listed as the registered publisher. Some authors care about this, but many don't as this is the most economical option. This does mean that you cannot then print the same paperback with another printer.

•The 'Expanded Distribution' system means that you do not have to only sell your printed book through the Amazon, but the book can also be shipped to the following channels: Bookstores and Online Retailers such as Barnes & Noble and to distributors such as Ingram and NACSCORP, Libraries and Academic Institutions through Baker & Taylor to libraries and academic institutions.

DISADVANTAGES OF USING KDP PRINT

• You have to know what you are doing with the interior design of your book, and although the website takes you through the formatting process, the quality of the finished book will depend on how well you understand and implement the detailed instructions.

• The Royalty Payment Schedule is a complex combination of several factors. The author receives the share of the sale after KDP Print has deducted their share. This is explained on the website, and there is a Royalty Calculator chart which clearly demonstrates that in order to make any income at all you need to minimise the number of pages in your manuscript and select your distribution channels very carefully.

• You will have to supply a PDF cover spread of your print book cover. This can be expensive.

If you would like more information on how to format your romance as a paperback book using Amazon KDP Print, I have created an in-depth step-by-step guide.

Find out more here>> https://www.amazon.com/dp/1798951320

PART SIX. MARKETING AND PROMOTION

24. Planning the Book Launch

It is all too easy to finish writing your story and instantly rush into loading it onto KDP so that it will be live and available for sale in a few hours.

That road leads to disillusionment, disappointment and frustration.

I know several romance authors who have almost given up writing because nobody bought the short book which they loved so much. Why? They rushed into the launch and it was a flop. Readers did not know that their book existed.

Please don't be one of those authors.

The most important thing that you can do to help readers find your work is to take the time to plan the book launch.

How long do you need to implement an effective book launch plan?

Take a deep breath.

Short Story: At least two weeks before the book goes live.

Novella or Short Novel: At least three to four weeks before the book goes live.

One of the advantages of self-publishing is that you are not driven by deadlines set by traditional publishers who have a tight fixed publication schedule – but those deadlines are brilliant tools to drive you forward.

From personal experience I would strongly recommend that you set yourself a fixed launch date and then work backwards from that date. In that way, you can be sure that all the steps on your book launch plan are in place and you focus on the writing.

TEMPLATE EBOOK LAUNCH PLAN

This is an example of a three-week eBook launch plan for a short novel or novella which you can adapt and extend or compress depending on your book and your launch schedule.

If you do skip steps, be aware of the impact this will have on the effectiveness of your launch.

HERE IS HOW IT WORKS.

The Launch Plan is triggered when you have the two components which you must have in place before you can publish a Kindle eBook:

1. A complete final draft of your manuscript, and

2. A book cover JPEG image.

FIRST LIMITING STEP. WRITING AND EDITING THE MANUSCRIPT

Work out how long it is going to take you to write and edit your book. Some authors will take a week perfecting a 7,000-word short story, while others can deliver an edited 30,000-word novella in two weeks and a 45,000 short novel in a month.

You are the only one who knows how long it will take. The writing process is different for everyone and your personal circumstances. If you only have one hour a day to write, this sets a constraint which should be worked into your launch plan.

Top tip? Don't give yourself too long. If you keep up the momentum this will drive the energy to carry your book launch forwards.

Always factor in the time needed for self-editing and proofreading which can take longer than you expect, especially is you have asked other people to edit your work.

This step sets the time limit for your launch plan which is triggered when the final draft is completed.

SECOND LIMITING STEP. YOUR BOOK COVER

Book cover design is an art form and will take at least a week. If you are on a tight budget for your short fiction, you can try a designer at Fiverr [maybe $30 for a premium eBook and print package] or a pre-made book cover from one of the many professional cover artists who specialise in romance covers [$50 plus]. The key thing is to focus on the genre expectations the audience will be expecting. An Historical Amish romance book cover will be different from a Paranormal Reverse Harem Shapeshifter erotic romance. Expect to have to compromise.

SIMPLE THREE-WEEK BOOK LAUNCH PLAN FOR A SHORT NOVEL OR NOVELLA

PRE-LAUNCH WEEK THREE

Set the Launch Date for your eBook. Write the date down on a sticky note and tape it to your computer or lap-top so that you can see it every day.

WRITING.

THE SELF-EDITING PROCESS STARTS THIS WEEK

Aim to take a step back and look at the overall shape of your story and where the main turning points are. Is there a clear character arc for both your hero and your heroine? Readers love it when the two main characters battle against real challenges before finally coming together.

CREATE A 'LEAD MAGNET' FREEBIE TO ADD TO YOUR BOOK

Create a lead magnet freebie on the same niche which could contain part of the main book or aligned content – available only to subscribers. Use this as the main reader magnet on blog posts and other promotional articles to get people to sign up for your email list. No hard pitching.

PUBLISHING.

Book Profile started in KDP

CATEGORIES AND KEYWORDS

Aim to incorporate keywords in the book title or subtitle if you can. Categories and keywords are selected for max impact and reach.

Research the best categories for this book if you haven't already done so. one top category for organic search and one less competitive category where you can rank higher and be listed in the top 20 front page.

THE BOOK DESCRIPTION

Use the language that the ideal reader would use.

The solution you are providing in this book must be in depth. Short, powerful and full of action steps. Package and design the book so that it is different and stands out and adds incredible value to the reader.

• Headline hook. Story Question. Problem. Conflict, Solution and benefits.

- Use bullets and short sentences so that it is scannable and irresistible.
- Use keywords if you can in the book description.
- Use limited HTML for bold and headers and lists. Test what it looks like using http://ablurb.github.io/

Save the book profile in Draft.

PRE-LAUNCH WEEK TWO

WRITING.

If you have time, send the book out to beta-readers. Ask them to be ruthless and pick out any plot or character problems as well as typos and come back to you within a week.

PUBLISHING.

THE BOOK COVER

Load the JPEG book cover onto KDP. Save the book profile in Draft.

KINDLE SELECT

Evaluate whether you are going make this eBook exclusive to the Kindle store.

MARKETING AND PROMOTION

PRE-LAUNCH EMAIL LIST BUILDING - CRUCIAL

Concept – build an audience of interested people before the launch rather than trying to sell and pitch to strangers.

If you have an email list, this is the time to recruit a Book Launch Team. The aim is to have a group of at least 20 email subscribers who commit to reading a free copy of your book in the next seven days and leave a review on the Amazon book page for your book.

PRE-LAUNCH WEEK ONE
WRITING.

Edit your manuscript and incorporate any changes suggested by beta-readers and proof-read the final text.

PUBLISHING.

FORMAT YOUR MANUSCRIPT FOR PUBLISHING ON KINDLE.

Format the text document for Kindle. Create a hyperlinked page of contents and front and back matter with links to reader magnets which will take them back to your site.

LOAD THE MANUSCRIPT ONTO KDP AND PREVIEW THE TEXT with the cover to make sure that the hyperlinked eBook table of contents, the links to your email list subscription and contact details are all working. Go back and edit the manuscript if you have to and reload. Download the file and check it on your kindle reader.

PRICING

Research and set the optimum launch price for your book.

Check that all the KDP book profile details are correct and launch your book on KDP. It usually loads overnight but it can take longer.

LAUNCHING WITH A FREE BOOK IN KINDLE SELECT

At this point you can decide to launch with a free promo for one or two days as part of Kindle Select. This is one way to deliver a free book to your email list subscribers rather than use a service like BookFunnel or InstaFreebie so that they can leave a review.

Be aware – when your book goes over to the Paid Amazon store, the ranking will start again.

MARKETING AND PROMOTION

Think about how you are going to promote the book.

Create nice graphics using Canva.com using your book cover and have them all ready for social media posts.

Pre-write any blog posts or media posts so that they flow from one site to another. Don't repeat the same thing on different sites.

SOFT LAUNCH – A FEW DAYS BEFORE THE BIG LAUNCH.

PUBLISHING

Once the book is live, check the Amazon Kindle store page for your book. Does the book description look okay or does it need to be updated? Do this now – it can take 48 hrs for the changes to go through. The "Look Inside" Feature can take a few days to be activated. As soon as it is live, check that the opening of your books is working well.

AMAZON AUTHOR CENTRAL

As soon as the eBook is live, you need to claim your book on Author Central on Amazon.com and any other author central stores you use. This can take a few hours to 24 hours after you add the book to your book list. When the book is loaded you can add in the editorial reviews, author notes and any other information you want for this book.

MARKETING AND PROMOTION

BOOK REVIEWS

Now that the book is live on the Kindle Store you can give all your email list subscribers the link to the book page.

Mention that it is now available at the launch price. Shamelessly ask them to buy a copy and leave a review if they enjoyed it. This would then be marked as a 'verified' review on Amazon.

Remind anyone who is on your Book Launch Team that they can now add their review of your book. Reviews provide social proof to readers browsing for books like yours.

GOODREADS

Claim your book on Goodreads if you have an author account and start engaging in reviews etc.

HARD BOOK LAUNCH

Ideally the main launch for your book should start when you have at least five good reviews and ideally a lot more.

Email the main email list again and let them know that the book is now live, and they can leave their review. Aim is to have lots of downloads and lots of reviews in next 48 hours.

Let them know that if they buy the book for 99 cents etc. this will be marked as a verified review and will not be stripped out by Amazon who has been cutting out reviews left without a purchase or made more difficulty to see.

MARKETING AND PROMOTION

• Share everywhere and be totally shameless!

• Start with your website or blog. Let the readers know how excited you are about your new release. Chat about the research and how much you enjoyed writing about this story.

• Write a blog post about "the ten best books in (your niche)". And link to your book at the same time. Then share the post everywhere – in that way it is not a direct sales pitch and the other authors might even share it to their audience.

• Give the link on every social media platform where you are active.

• Do a cover reveal everywhere, especially Twitter. Linking to the book. Facebook has limited organic reach these days, but it does recognise posts which are shared or linked.

• Ask all your author pals to share the news [you will do the same for them] and give them the link to the Amazon book page.

Be aware that there is a lag time between book sales and Amazon reports, so don't be too worried if you don't see sales in the first 24 hours after the book goes live.

POST LAUNCH
Review what worked and what didn't. You may need to change categories or re-write the book description.

Paid advertising can be a game changer for a series – but I would strongly recommend keeping to a low budget and focusing on books which have at least ten good reviews.

25. Author Branding

MARKETING AND PROMOTION

Readers have to know that your short Kindle romance exists, so you should plan in advance to spend an intensive period of promotion during the first weeks after your book goes live on the Kindle store. But it does pay to think of using your time and energy strategically.

REVIEWS HELP TO SELL BOOKS

Many debut romance authors set a very low list price when they launch their eBook or offer it for a free during a short promotional window. This used to be a very effective way of attracting large numbers of downloads and a few reviews, but just because someone downloaded your eBook, this does not mean that they have read it or are going to review it.

This is where your social media connections come into force. Let your friends and followers know that your romance is going to be available at a special promotional price for a certain period and that you would love them to take advantage of the offer, especially if they could leave a review.

Once you have at least five good reviews, then you can extend your reach and go for a more intensive promotional campaign. Your book reviews help browsers to the Kindle store to feel comfortable that they are not going to waste their time or money when they purchase your romance eBook.

YOUR AUTHOR BRAND AND READER EXPECTATION

Most career authors have found that once they have published several romance novels or other formats in one particular romance subgenre, then their author name becomes associated with that subgenre.

They can build up a following of fans and create an audience for their work.

For example: If I mentioned the name **E. L. James,** then most readers familiar with her debut work "The Fifty Shades of Grey" would expect a book with her name on the cover to have a certain combination of contemporary romance and erotica elements which make up her brand.

This is why some romance authors write under more than one name, so that they are not creatively inhibited from writing in more than one classification of fiction.

With the increased interaction between readers and authors using the power of the Internet, this situation is slowly changing but you should understand that most romance authors choose to build up a following of readers in one particular subgenre for business reasons before writing in another subgenre.

26. Amazon Author Central

The next step is to **Add Your Book** to your book list on your local Amazon Author Central account.

Amazon Author Central should already have your author profile:

• your professional author photograph

• your interesting biography and achievements, including any awards or contests

• links to your website and social media connections. Linking your blog adds another level of connection between your author brand and your readers. Video content can really help to grab a reader's attention.

This profile will be displayed with every book on sale on the Kindle Store, so this is a powerful way to convey your professionalism and credentials to any prospective buyer of your book.

When your eBook goes live on Amazon you can add that eBook to your author profile and add exclusive 'Editorial' Review content which Amazon will publish on the Kindle Store page for that book. Amazon does your marketing for you!

Always link to your Amazon author page in the back of your books so that readers will be directed to your full book list

27. Email List Building for Romance Authors

An email list of subscribers who love your work is an extremely valuable, long-term asset you can use for years to promote your books, increase sales, build your authority in your niche and develop a real connection with your readers.

Instead of sending social media posts about your latest release, sharing the news with engaged subscribers on an email list can help your books to become instant bestsellers.

What three things are you trying to achieve by sending out a newsletter to the subscribers who have joined your email list?

#Build a relationship with readers

#Offer them special promotions and giveaways

#Offer them some bonus in exchange for their support when your next book launches.

In other words – **it is ALL about the subscribers** and what they want and expect from you.

SO HOW CAN YOU LEVERAGE THE POWER OF YOUR AUTHOR NEWSLETTER?

Most readers are thinking and asking: What's in it for me? Why should I take the time to open this email?

You display authority in your customer's eyes when you demonstrate that you have a deep and practical understanding of their needs and desires, based on your own personal experience.

Think of your email newsletter as the equivalent of a one to one conversation that you have with someone who you are meeting in person.

1. DELIVER ON WHAT YOU PROMISED

When someone subscribed to your email list you may have offered them a welcome gift in the form of a free digital product, or some kind of giveaway in exchange for their contact details.

If you promised your subscriber updates about new releases then share the journey you are going on to develop your latest project, so that they are excited to see your cover reveal and ready to support you when your book is released.

Offer them an exclusive advanced extract – just for subscribers.

Invite them to join the launch team and become a beta-reader for your next book. Ask your reader to leave a book review in exchange for a free advance copy and share the news about the launch.

2. OFFERS, FREEBIES, CONTESTS AND GIVEAWAYS

Offering free and discounted books and physical products or services can create a big increase in your email subscribers. Take care to engage with these new subscribers and make sure that you are offering them real education and information from the start.

Always make sure that your existing subscribers don't feel left out and offer them some free books or other giveaway.

3. BE CONSISTENT

If you promised that you would send out a weekly or monthly newsletter, then you should commit to sending that email on time.

You are going to get a lot of un-subscribers if you only send out a single email every few months when your new book is released and nothing in between. All pitch, pitch, pitch. *Buy my book, buy my book.* That is a very *one-sided* conversation.

Decide on how often you are going to email out your author newsletter and then stick to that schedule.

BE HUMAN AND AUTHENTIC

You want to make your reader looks forward to hearing from you.

One of the most effective ways of doing this is by sharing your own personal life story. It does not have to be a "zero to hero" story where you list impressive numbers and achievements.

In fact, it can be better for the reader to empathise and sympathise with you if they recognise that you are someone who struggles with and has overcome the same challenges as they have in their life.

We all make mistakes. Have fun with it and share anecdotes and stories when things did not go to plan.

BE POSITIVE AND INSPIRATIONAL IF YOU CAN

There is enough negativity in the world without your readers having to read about it in your emails.

Imagine that you are a published author and you meet a reader at a conference and they start chatting in a friendly manner over coffee and they ask you what you are up to lately.

Scenario One.

You pull out a copy of your latest self-published book and start reading out the book descriptions and reviews from your entire back catalogue from your Kindle.

Then you start rambling on about the state of the publishing industry in general and all your woes and how much you hate publicity and having to do promotions. In fact, you are so fed up with having to write so much to make a living and how miserable you are, that you are thinking of going back to the "day job".

Scenario Two.

You smile and laugh and say that you are having the best time. People are so generous. You have been amazed about how well your last book was received. And the reviews are so kind.

It is really encouraging, and you cannot wait to get started on the next book in the series and meeting up with your favourite characters again and find out what has been happing in their lives.

Which option do you think your ideal reader wants to listen to and read?

DON'T REPEAT WHAT YOU HAVE JUST SAID ON SOCIAL MEDIA.

Social media has its place in any author platform, but it cannot replace the one to one connection that comes from sending a personal email to your subscribers and engaging them in conversation.

Subscribers want to know more than just your blog and publishing schedule. They have subscribed to receive information that they cannot find on social media or your blog or website. They want to connect with you as a person.

Be creative and share fun content that relates to you and your book and connects with your readers on a more personal level.

For example, what books are you reading at the moment, or a review of a movie that you enjoyed. Tell an anecdote about something that happened to you in real life and your reaction and learning experience. If you keep it lighthearted and fun, the readers will look forward to receiving your emails.

Many authors are reluctant to share photos of their private home on social media but will do so in a newsletter, including images of their family and pets, holiday moments and their personal bookshelves. This builds that all-important engagement with your readers who will come to know, like and trust you.

Don't forget – they love reading the same kind of romance that you love to read and write. They are your tribe!

SHARE EXCLUSIVE INSIGHTS INTO YOUR LIFE AND YOUR WORK

What are you working on right now?

What is your working process?

Are you someone who thrives on chaos and noise and loves to work in a busy coffee shop? Or perhaps you are the exact opposite. You need a calm and quiet space, free of distractions, before you can engage in any sort of creative thinking.

Share that with the readers and let them know if you have an image gallery, music playlist or a special screensaver that instantly takes your back into the world of your book, whether fiction or non-fiction.

Don't forget to share news about other projects and public events, conferences, guest posting, podcasts interviews and media presentations.

ALWAYS INCLUDE ONE SPECIFIC ACTION THAT YOUR READER SHOULD TAKE IN EVERY EMAIL.

This "Call to Action" could be as simple as a link to your latest blog post or podcast interview, or a link to the sales page for your latest release.

Always ask your readers to reply to your emails.

A one-way conversation is boring. At the end of every email newsletter, pose at least one question. It could be related to the topic of your book or about the genre of your work in general.

If you have posted about a specific piece of research that you have carried out, such as a setting for a novel or a new gluten-free cooking regime, then ask if they enjoyed hearing about this subject. Do they have any ideas for other topics?

Surveys and polls.

Ask your readers what they like and would like to see more of. Then deliver it! You can use SurveyMonkey or other free online survey forms and integrate them into the email. Be sure to come back to your subscribers in a later newsletter and share the results of the survey. If there is a particularly interesting reply, answer the subscriber with a personal email.

THINK ABOUT THE MEDIUM

Many readers will scan their emails on their mobile phones when they can snatch a few precious minutes in their daily life.

• We are all busy and expect emails to be short and to the point. Not rambling essays which are not mobile friendly.

• Long text emails which appear very "dense" and difficult to navigate will not be opened.

• Use an appealing subject line which encourages your reader to open the email.

• Break your email up into sections with scannable headings and subheadings and one or two images.

• Add a summary of your key information in the last paragraph with the specific "Call to Action" you want your reader to take after reading the email.

CONSIDER USING IMAGES AND VIDEO

In most cases you want the option to have an image of your book cover in your newsletter and possibly in the header of your email.

Romance readers are familiar with very visual promotional material used by the beauty and fashion industry, so your newsletter could have lots of images in a magazine format, with multiple columns which will appeal to your particular niche audience.

You can embed a video inside your email, but if you want to include a video in your newsletter, it is better to add an Image to the email and then hyperlink that image to the web address of a video which is hosted on another site such as YouTube or a video service such as Vimeo or Wistia etc. That keeps your email "clean" and easy to read.

DON'T UNDERESTIMATE THE POWER OF A SIMPLE NEWSLETTER. IT CAN SERIOUSLY GROW YOUR BUSINESS.

Building an email list of engaged subscribers has never been more important.

Your email list is an asset which you have control over and can retain and nurture for the long term. Not a six-second video clip.

The only limit to your content is your own creativity.

This is why a simple newsletter is one of the best ways to grow a long-term career as an author and build the community and culture of your brand.

50 CONTENT IDEAS FOR YOUR AUTHOR NEWSLETTER

Go HERE for 50 Inspiring Ideas for Your Author Newsletter>>

https://ninaharrington.com/wp-content/uploads/2019/04/50-Content-Ideas-for-your-Author-Newsletter.pdf

CREATE A BOOK LAUNCH ADVANCE READER TEAM

Five days before target launch date, invite your email subscribers, or friends if you don't have an email list, to be part of the Book Launch Team.

Ask if anyone on your existing email list of subscribers would be interested in receiving a free review copy of the book.

You then ask them to read the book when you have an ARC [advanced reading copy] available and leave the review during launch week.

Then send them the review copy by BookFunnel, Instafreebie or directly by email.

HOW TO CREATE ARCS OF YOUR BOOK.

Create an ARC folder for this book on your computer.

Then open your final book master text and save a copy with the word ARC in front of the title into this folder.

How to create a PDF of your book.

Insert the book cover to the front page of your manuscript in Microsoft Word, then save as a PDF, or if you are using Word 2016, Export to PDF.

How to create a Kindle eBook ARC.

Download a copy of the preview Kindle mobi file from KDP onto your computer.

It can be very useful to create a special ARC version of your final book.

Insert a new page in the Front Matter, such as just before Chapter One, and write a note just for your book launch team;

- Thanking them for being so generous with their time and agreeing to read the book over the next few days.
- Reminding them it would be super if they could leave their review on or soon after the [specific launch date]
- Asking them to report back any typos or errors that they spot by email with a location number or chapter etc.
- Give them a link to the book page on Amazon where they can write the review. You can include Goodreads if you are active on it.
- Point them to the Pre-order page in every email. Shamelessly ask them to leave a review.

Hopefully you might get a 10% response. Maybe less. So, aim for a launch team of at least 60 if possible – those 20 reviews in launch week make a huge difference.

28. Free Marketing Tools and Techniques

CONSIDER WRITING A SERIES OF BOOKS AND MORE OF THEM

The good news is that shorter books and linked series of romances are selling well. Romance novellas and linked novellas are perfect for the time stretched romance reader.

Many very successful contemporary romance authors have shifted to writing one or two longer romance novels a year, but also a linked series of novellas. You can then release the novella individually and as a bundle later in the year.

OFFER THE FIRST BOOK IN THE SERIES AS PERMANENTLY FREE

If you offer the first book in the series as permanently free or at very low cost, then this will feed interest in the rest of the series and build long term sales. Use the back of each book to link into the other titles in the series and make sure that your blog or website tells your fans when the new release is out.

What is more, your name will dominate that Kindle Store shelf and bring in new readers as your catalogue grows, which taps into the Amazon marketing systems.

HOW DO YOU SET YOUR BOOK PERMANENTLY FOR FREE ON AMAZON?

Amazon will not allow you to set a price of zero for your book, so the only way you can give your book away is by publishing for free on another site and asking Amazon to price match.

You only want to do this when you have other books available for sale at full price.

At the end of your 90 days on Kindle Select, take your book out of Kindle Select and publish it on one or more of the other publishing platforms, such as Draft to Digital, Smashwords, Kobo and iTunes and set the price for free.

To do this you will need to create an ePUB version of your book and register on the other bookstores. Amazon will then price match when you publish the same book on other platforms, but you must tell them about it.

You do this by going into your KDP dashboard and clicking on the Contact button. Email Amazon and give them the links to your book when it is live on the other platforms for free and ask them to set the price for your Kindle book at zero.

Amazon recognise that a free book in a series is a great way of selling your other Kindle books at full price, but it may take a few days for the price to change.

Many authors have used a permanently free book as a way of drawing readers to their website so that they can collect email addresses, or to persuade them to try the other books in the series.

The Pre-Launch Promotion Campaign then switches to a Soft Launch Campaign. What do I mean by Soft Launch?

SOFT LAUNCH.

A $0.99 [£0.99] book launch where reviewers can leave reviews on the live platform. Free ARC available on BookFunnel or InstaFreebie or direct from your email list.

Then wait a week or so until you have at least ten good reviews and hopefully a lot more. Ideal target is 20 reviews.

Then switch over to the Hard Launch at the same price.

HARD LAUNCH PROMOTION PLAN

All the focus is on the book you want to launch. You must drive traffic and visibility.

There are basically two ways people can discover your book.

FREE. Either they are going onto Amazon or on Google and searching for your kind of book. Hopefully your book will come up.

PAID. The alternative is that you have to pay to be on someone's email list or search results, so you will have to pay for advertisements.

TEN FREE PROMOTIONAL TOOLS

#1. Blog Posts. One blog post announcing the release. Then share that announcement everywhere. Write this blog post in advance.

#2. Blog Posts linked to the book.

At least three blog posts about the book and the topics and themes every day over the next two weeks. All linked to the new book. But no direct pitching or sales. Make it useful. Recipes. Local area research. Behind the scenes on the character. Just adding a simple link to the book page on Amazon at the end.

Write these blog posts in advance and have them ready to go. Create nice graphics with your book cover to use as the feature image for the post. Then share that post with relevant Facebook groups where you are a member and use relevant Twitter hashtags to increase reach.

#3. Social Media.

PLUS - Share the success of the launch every day on social and to pals etc. Just chatty and friendly. No pitching or hard selling. I use Facebook and Twitter.

Draft the text for these out in advance. Create nice simple graphics with your book cover which catch the eye.

#4. Friends and writing groups.

Shamelessly share how excited you are about the launch and ask them to share with their lists and online platform – give them the link to your announcement post or social media post with a nice graphic. Offer to do the same for their next book launch, as you have done before of course.

#5. Email List Subscribers.

They should already know all about the launch since they have supported you from the start. Now is the time to thank them for their support, remind them to leave a review and to share the announcement with their pals.

#6. Niche Facebook Groups.

If you have been sharing your progress with selected Facebook groups relevant to your niche, let them know how things are going and share the link. No hard sales pitching – be useful and relevant. Make a list of all of the Facebook groups where you are active so that you don't miss any.

#7. 99 cents Facebook Groups.

You already have the graphics and text, so it only takes minutes to share the Facebook post with bargain hungry readers.

Make a list of all the 99 cents and Kindle 99 cents Facebook groups now. If you are running a free launch for a few days, do the same thing – there are lots of free Kindle book groups.

#8. **Add an Amazon Affiliate Banner** advert on your website.

MURDER AND MOZZARELLA...
$0.99
Shop now

If you are signed up for the Amazon affiliate programme, you can link your book to Amazon using a text link or add the text and image code into a widget on your website which will display a one-click purchase link to your book.

Affiliate links are only allowed from your website. Everywhere else you must Link to Amazon Page for Book – use the direct link that ends in the ASIN – not an affiliate link which is against terms of service if is not on my website.

#9. Use technology to make it easier to spread the world.

"Today's the day! My new book is live on Amazon and just $0.99 for a limited time. Grab a copy and feel free to around. Link =

Use http://hrefshare.com/

People often need to see your promotion <u>seven times or more</u> before they actually remember to take advantage of it. To save time, you can used automation and amplification tools like MeetEdgar, CoPromote, Buffer, and Hootsuite to get as much scheduled in advance as possible.

#10. Create eye-catching graphics and visuals for every promotion.

BOOK ONE. MURDER AND MOZZARELLA

The 1st book in the NEW Kingsmede Cozy Mystery series is out now! Only 99c/99p on Kindle or FREE on #KindleUnlimited! Also available as a paperback!

US: https://www.amazon.com/dp/B0791J3HCF

UK: https://www.amazon.co.uk/dp/B0791J3HCF

How to Create the Promotional Graphics - FREE

Derek Murphy from Creative Indie has shared a super useful range of PowerPoint and Google Slides which anyone can easily modify, simply by replacing the cover image. There is also a YouTube video telling you how to do it.

http://www.creativindie.com/how-to-design-3d-book-promotional-graphics-with-google-slides-free-templates/

https://www.youtube.com/watch?v=4DaOe5Nj4WU&t=8s

Save that specific slide as an image, and you can use it to promote your work anywhere.

This is one example for book one in the series.

How to Create the 3-D Book Image - FREE

I followed the instructions here>
http://www.myebook.co.za/how-to-make-a-free-3d-cover-image-of-your-book

You will need Flash to open the editor, then follow the instructions, download the 3-D image provided, paste your book cover on top as a layer and drag the corners to fit over the 3-D image. Save as an image.

I used this 3-D image in the PowerPoint slides and on other graphics in Canva.

29. Paid Marketing Services

PAID PROMOTIONAL TOOLS

Sometimes organic reach is not enough, and it is worth investing in paid promotions to reach out and get the attention of more ideal readers for your book.

Usually the cost of these ads means that you should only run them if you have a short novel or are trying to expand your reach and introduce your work to new readers.

There are three main types of paid advertisements used by authors:

- **Facebook Ads.**
- **Amazon Advertising**
- **Book Promotion Websites**

FACEBOOK ADS

My opinion, based on what I have read and seen, is that Facebook adverts are great when you have a series of at least three books already live. The high promotional costs for books one and two are offset by the sales of all the other great books in the rest of the series plus page reads on Kindle Unlimited.

In addition, Facebook ads are a form of interruption marketing. Readers come onto Facebook to be social and interact with friends and followers and will ignore ads for books or get annoyed by them.

That's why I would recommend being very careful about using Facebook Messenger marketing. I'm sure that I am not the only one who has received messages from authors asking you to buy their book. This is spam, spam, spam = unfollow, block and report. Of course, this is just my opinion and there are people who use these systems very effectively.

In general, most authors who are successful with Facebook ads wait until all three or more books are live with good reviews and then evaluate whether they are worth it or not to give a boost to sales post-launch.

AMAZON ADVERTISING

Amazon ads offer a really exciting opportunity for self-published authors. In contrast to Facebook, readers come to Amazon actively looking for books to purchase.

They want recommendations and may at least click on your book and take a look. If you have a great cover and book description, there is a chance that you could covert that browser into a buyer.

Most short romance fiction is priced between 99 cents and $2.99 for a short novel, so there is no guaranteed that it is going to be cost effective to pay to promote a book at that price. The only way to find out is to experiment with low daily budgets and monitor the results.

My personal experience so far is that I can usually break even or make money from book sales with Amazon ads.

HOW TO USE AMAZON ADS.

Amazon ads are cost-per-click, meaning you only pay when shoppers click on your ad. The minimum budget to run an ad is $1/day or $100 per campaign, depending on the ad type you choose.

Most authors prefer to use Sponsored Ads.

Be prepared to experiment and check the results in hard sales/ranking/clicks. You can start with a few dollars a day for a week and change the keywords until they perform well.

The two common criticisms of AMS are that the reporting is poor and unreliable, and it can very difficult to budget, since Amazon is unlikely to spend the amount you have allocated. On the flip side, you can several campaigns and compare the results using the keywords that Amazon suggests, with your own chosen niche keywords. If you are looking for ideal readers in a specific niche – then this is the option to select.

Amazon Marketing Services have good tutorials which you can find here> https://advertising.amazon.com/kdp-authors

BOOK PROMOTION WEBSITES

There are many options available in 2020, but some of the more popular sites include:

Bargain Booksy. https://www.bargainbooksy.com/sell-more-books/

ENT. http://ereadernewstoday.com/requirements/

AskDavid.com

Book Barbarian

Choosy Bookworm.

The largest and by far the most expensive is BookBub.

For example, the Book Bub Contemporary Romance group has over two million subscribers worldwide.

If only a small percentage of Book Bub readers join your email list from the link inside the book on offer, this could be a very cost-effective way of building an email list of readers for your next book.

BookBub deal could work well for a promo of the first 99 cents book in the series when you have at least 3 books written. The acceptance criteria make it clear that they are looking for books with good reviews, so it is not designed for book launch for the first book in a series.

Featured Deals may be booked up to 30 days in advance at the prices currently displayed, and they are well known to be very picky.

OTHER PAID OPTIONS

These are only a few of the more popular PAID promotional opportunities for authors - they are many more available, both online and off-line. For example; If you have created a paperback book, you can buy author copies and hand sell at events or gift them to reviewers.

WRITE MORE BOOKS

You have invested so much time and energy and probably money creating, crafting, publishing and promoting your work. For me, the best way that I can leverage that investment is to write more books that readers will want to read and then share those books with the largest audience possible.

POST LAUNCH MARKETING

BOOK REVIEWS

Depending on the length of your book and how much notice you gave your targeted list, it may take a few weeks before these readers come back with a book review on Amazon, if they come back at all.

In the interim you are going to have to depend on the organic growth of your sales as readers find your eBook and come back with reviews, good or bad.

This can take weeks.

Building awareness and interest in both you author brand and your work in the first few weeks following a launch is a great way to make sure that your book has the best chance of exposure to readers.

FREE, PHASED AND FULL PRICE

Many authors decide to adopt a two-phase pricing strategy and launch their book for free, or at a low price to encourage readers who want a low-risk option.

To launch, set the price to free, if you are in Kindle Select, 99 cents, or $1.99 if it is a longer novel in a popular subgenre.

The phase two, full price band kicks in, when the book has at least ten good reviews on the book page and the book ranking has held or improved because of the additional downloads.

AFTER THE LAUNCH MONTH

Be prepared that marketing does not stop when your book is launched. Just the opposite. Promoting any book is a marathon not a sprint.

After your book has been on sale for a few months and the sales ranking starts to fall, if you have positive reviews and plenty of them, it is always worth boosting the sales again with a free book promotion.

Some authors do this before their 90-day compulsory window on Kindle Select expires, so that they get the benefit of the additional Amazon sales but then decide not to renew on Kindle and release their book on other platforms.

This is a tricky decision and you must look carefully at the sales data and the income reports.

For example, do you have a lot of downloads from Kindle Unlimited? How much is this worth to you? The monthly fund for Kindle Unlimited does vary of course.

Will you gain more sales on Kobo and iBooks and other platforms to compensate for the loss of these sales?

This is particularly important when you have created a series of short romance books and want to launch the next book in the series. Building a following on one platform can be a great way of developing an audience and growing your email list.

MORE RESOURCES FROM NINA

SUBSCRIBE HERE TO RECEIVE A FREE DIGITAL DOWNLOAD

THE 16-CHAPTER ROMANCE PLOT OUTLINE

A Complete Template with everything you need to Plot your own unique Romance Fiction.

HOW TO WRITE SHORT ROMANCE KINDLE BOOKS — A COMPLETE GUIDE TO KINDLE PUBLISHING — NINA HARRINGTON

Download a Free Text Copy of the 16-Chapter Romance Plot Template as a Welcome Gift when you Subscribe to my Newsletter.

Find out more here:
https://subscribepage.io/16CHAPTEROUTLINE

ABOUT NINA HARRINGTON

Nina Harrington writes fun, award winning contemporary romance for the Harlequin, single title romantic mysteries, and best-selling guides and training courses for authors. Over 1.6 million of Nina's books have been sold in over 28 countries and translated into 23 languages.

Find out more about Nina at: htts://www.ninaharrington.com.

Before you go, thank you for purchasing this copy of: HOW TO WRITE SHORT ROMANCE KINDLE BOOKS.

If you enjoyed it and found it useful, please help other readers find this book by writing a review of this book on your local Amazon Store. Thank you!

COPYRIGHT

HOW TO WRITE SHORT ROMANCE KINDLE BOOKS.

A Complete Guide to Kindle Direct Publishing

Published by NinaHarringtonDigital

Copyright (©) 2023 by Nina Harrington

ISBN: 9781982931094

This book is licensed for your personal enjoyment only. This book may not be re-sold or given away to other people. Thank you for respecting the hard work of the author. To obtain permission to excerpt portions of the text, please contact the author at: https://ninaharrington.com/

In preparing this book I carried out extensive research and give credit to the original author when appropriate. Please note this is a constantly changing publishing landscape where companies and policies change without notice. You should always carry out your own research to obtain the latest information.

Amazon, Kindle, and all related logos are trademarks of Amazon.com, Inc. and its affiliates. Kindle Create and Kindle Direct Publishing are registered trademarks of Amazon.com, Inc. and its affiliates. This book is not endorsed or authorised by Amazon.com, Inc. or its affiliates.

Please note that the spelling and grammar in this book are UK English.

FAST-TRACK GUIDES
FOCUSED TRAINING FOR AUTHORS

Made in United States
Troutdale, OR
03/14/2024